Joseph Broeckaert

Life of the Blessed Charles Spinola, of the Society of Jesus

Joseph Broeckaert

Life of the Blessed Charles Spinola, of the Society of Jesus

ISBN/EAN: 9783337168971

Printed in Europe, USA, Canada, Australia, Japan

Cover: Foto ©ninafisch / pixelio.de

More available books at **www.hansebooks.com**

OF THE

BLESSED CHARLES SPINOLA,

OF THE SOCIETY OF JESUS:

WITH A SKETCH OF THE OTHER JAPANESE MARTYRS BEATIFIED
ON THE 7TH OF JULY, 1867.

BY

JOSEPH BROECKAERT, S. J.

New York:
JOHN G. SHEA.
1869.

Entered according to act of Congress, in the year 1868,

By JOSEPH LOYZANCE,

In the Clerk's Office of the District Court of the United States, for the Southern District of New York.

PREFACE.

In the month of December, 1866, when the French, on leaving Rome, seemed to abandon the Pope to the mercy of his enemies, all eyes were riveted on the holy city, in the expectation of some revolutionary movement. This was the moment chosen by Pius IX to announce to the astonished world that, in the month of July then ensuing, he would solemnly proceed to the Beatification of a large number of Japanese martyrs. As this coincided with the time for celebrating the eighteenth centenary jubilee of the death of St. Peter, the Sovereign Pontiff invited all the bishops of Catholicity to gather around him on that occasion. Some regarded this as a challenge; it was, however, simply a holy confidence in the cause of the Church; it was, perhaps, an inspiration from on High. In spite of menacing forebodings, in spite of dark plots, all took place as the Pope had announced, and the august ceremony of the glorification of our martyrs was accomplished with a splendor of which Rome alone is capable, and was witnessed by five hundred bishops and thousands of the faithful from all parts of the world. Praised be Jesus Christ! He watches over his Church, while he tries it; he justifies his promises, and guarantees them anew to the end of time.

Japanese martyrs! Twice within a few years we behold Saints from the far East glorified, and while we render this homage to the martyrs of the seventeenth century, other combats crimson the same soil, illustrious confessors suffer and die for the faith, new crowns are woven for new triumphing heroes. Must the blood of martyrs be again the seed of Christians? Is the Gospel to conquer the rest of heathendom? Will the torch of faith fade from the eyes of ungrateful races to enlighten those still seated in the shadow of death? This is God's secret. Bowing to his inscrutable designs, let us celebrate with joy the triumph of the Japanese martyrs; let us, with Pius IX., confidently invoke their support in the tribulations amid which the Holy Church of Christ is passing.

The Beatified servants of God proclaimed in the solemnity of July 7, 1867, number two hundred and five. They comprise religious of the orders of St. Dominic and St. Francis, Augustinians, Jesuits, and many Japanese laics.[1] Among these groups of glori-

---

[1] Of the two hundred and five martyrs there are twenty-one Dominicans, eighteen Franciscans, five Augustinians, and thirty-three Members of the Society of Jesus. It will also be consoling to see that several are by their birth or apostolic labors identified with America.

ous martyrs there is one which must especially rivet the attention of a son of St. Ignatius, and at the head of this group[1] stands a holy personage in whom the author of this book has for forty years vowed special confidence. Now that he can, in all freedom, unite his voice to that of the Supreme Head of the Church, he would be happy, indeed, if he can infuse into all the children of God the same sentiments; more happy still, if the perusal of these pages inspire some elect souls with a devotedness like that of the holy martyr.

The life of Father Charles Spinola was written in Italian only six years after his death, by his cousin, Father Fabius Ambrose Spinola. In every respect it deserves implicit confidence, and has been used by all who have treated of the same subject. Father Herman Hugo translated it into Latin, and Father d'Orleans gave an abridgment of it in French. Besides this principal source I have consulted the History of Japan by Father de Charlevoix; Father Cordara's Sixth Part of the Latin History of the Society of Jesus, the Letters of St. Francis Xavier, and some other "Indian Letters," without enumerating the modern publications on the Japanese martyrs.

In selecting a hero among the illustrious men whom the Church has just placed on our altars, I

---

[1] May one of the translators add that, on his part, he learned to venerate Blessed Charles Spinola from Father Isaac Jogues, who died for the faith in New York State, and who had taken B. Charles as the patron of his missionary career.

cannot entirely pass over the glorious deaths of his companions. Moreover, I was so delighted with what I have just read in the Italian account by Father Boero, the zealous postulator in the cause of the Beatification, that I have deemed it proper to add to this life of Blessed Charles Spinola an account of the two hundred and five martyrs beatified July 7, 1867.

The portrait given is taken from that issued from Plantin's press in 1630, and may be considered as authentic. It was doubtless the one used in the miraculous cures to be mentioned hereafter. The plan of the prison of Omura is from a design of the Blessed Charles himself transmitted by him to Rome. The group of martyrs is reproduced from a remarkable painting used in the ceremony of the Beatification.

LOUVAIN, NATIVITY OF OUR LORD, 1867.

INTRODUCTION.

I.

PERSECUTIONS OF THE CHURCH IN JAPAN.

The Church of Japan, though of a recent foundation, has been one of the most illustrious by the examples of unshaken constancy in the faith which it has exhibited. The apostle St. Francis Xavier, first in 1549, bore the light of the gospel to that remote empire; for twenty-seven months he visited the principal cities, penetrating to Macao, its capital, amid a thousand dangers, with incalculable hardship, but he converted to Christianity a great number of proselytes, whom he confided to the care and zeal of his successors. So rapidly did Christianity spread during the reign of Nobunanga, and the first five years of that of Taicosama, that there were more than two hundred thousand Catholics in the various kingdoms of the island. But in 1596 Taicosama inaugurated the era of persecution. It was this first general persecution that gave the martyrs' palm to the twenty-six who died on the cross at Nangasaki, February 5, 1597. Their death was followed by some quiet, and according to the relations of the missionaries of the Society of Jesus, they converted and baptized no less than two hundred and four thousand idolaters in the next eight years.

After Taicosama's death, Daifusama, guardian of Findeiori, lawful heir of the crown, seized the throne, and, by the terror of his arms, reduced all the Japanese princes. At first this emperor showed no hostility to the Christians; he even showed them favor; but when he beheld himself firmly seated on the throne, he became their open persecutor. In the year 1614, after banishing from his court the Christian princes and lords and confiscating their property, he published an edict, throughout all Japan, commanding the immediate demolition of the churches, religious houses, hospitals and other similar institutions, as well as the destruction by fire of crosses, pictures and religious books. The ministers of the Gospel were to leave the country by a specified day; all who professed the law of Christ were to renounce it and return to the worship of the gods of the country. Those who were obstinate or contumacious were to be condemned, without remission, to lose their property and life, their houses to be demolished and their families destroyed. The same penalty was extended to all who harbored priests or Christians, and even to those who knew of their place of concealment but did not denounce it. Xongun his son, and Toxungun his grandson, who in turn succeeded him, confirmed these laws, adding others of still greater cruelty.

The persecution lasted more than thirty years, and

ended in the almost utter ruin of this flourishing church. As the tyrants invented more barbarous torments, the faithful displayed greater courage in enduring them. It was a common thing to crush a martyr with maces, pierce his flesh with red hot irons, hang him on a cross, cut off part of his head. The executioners added incredible refinements of barbarity. They tore with pincers the skin, limbs, muscles and nerves of the martyr; his flesh was cut off morsel by morsel with dull knives; some were dipped naked in icy waters, others burnt for two or three hours by a slow fire; they were plunged slowly into boiling sulphur springs, which made their flesh one ulcer, and filled it with worms as though that of decaying corpses.

In spite of these horrible torments the Christians displayed the wonderful spectacle of a courage superior to every trial. They were seen preparing for martyrdom, esteeming themselves happy to sacrifice their lives for the law of Jesus Christ. Nor was it only the lower walks of life, the robust classes, who gave these examples of intrepidity; they were found in noblemen, belonging to royal families, nurtured amid the ease and luxuries of life, in aged women, in delicate girls, and even in children. In this noble career the way was led by the Catholic missionaries, ministers of God, preachers of the Gospel, come from Italy, Spain, Portugal, Mexico, only to gain souls to Christ and close untold labors by this painful martyrdom. They belonged to the religious orders of St. Dominic, St. Francis, St. Augustine and to the Society of Jesus.

Many were men of mark, by the nobility of their race or the extent of their learning, and especially by their heroic virtue and the laborious exercise of their apostleship. All, moreover, religious and laymen, natives of Japan or of other lands, Christians of more or less recent date, undeterred by the sight of torments—on the contrary rushed forward to them. They were seen eagerly enrolling their names in the lists of the condemned, and then sure of dying for Christ, they don their finest dresses, to appear with joy and intrepidity before their judges, answer them boldly, thank their executioners, preach from their very crosses, and sing amid the flames. Mothers were seen offering their children to death and asking greater torments for them. These wonders were evident miracles of divine grace like those wrought by God on the martyrs of the primitive church, in confirmation of our faith. Hence ecclesiastical historians and the apologists of religion unhesitatingly adduce, as a proof of the divinity of Catholicity, the constancy of the Japanese martyrs.

The victims of the persecution numbered many thousands. Of many, precise and definite accounts were drawn up from the accounts of missionaries from time to time, from the statements of Japanese exiles, and from the testimony of Spanish and Portuguese merchants.

Meanwhile the persecution went steadily on, and in 1639 all Europeans, except the Dutch, were excluded from Japan, even for trade, and Portuguese ambassadors sent to the island were beheaded. In 1642 five

Jesuit Fathers landed secretly, but were soon discovered and put to death.

The last known entrance of a missionary was that of a Sicilian priest, named Sidotti, who landed in October, 1709, but was soon arrested and taken to Yedo. After remaining in prison several years and converting many who came to him, he was walled up in a close cell, four or five feet deep, and fed through a small aperture till he died.

Subsequent efforts were equally ineffectual. To all appearance Christianity was crushed completely in Japan. But God in his providence had not allowed so many martyrs to die in vain. They had preserved the faith of thousands.

The following, from the Annals of the Propagation of the Faith, will give the best idea of the present state of the Church in Japan:

II.

One of the last acts of Gregory XVI. was the erection, in 1846, of Japan and the archipelago of Lew Chew into a vicariate-apostolic. The Rev. Mgr. Augustus Forcade, of the Foreign Missions, who, for two years, had been established at Lew Chew as an outpost, was charged with the new Mission. With regard to the state of religion in Japan at that time, we have the following account from the Vicar-Apostolic, dated Macao, January 25, 1847 : "Japan still remains inaccessible, impenetrable; as of old, her kings have stood up and her princes assembled against the Lord and his Christ; the present differs nothing from the past, and were a Missioner to attempt to enter the country, there is no doubt he would be immediately discovered, and at once struck down. Considering the state of things, therefore, in a human point of view, our work appears simply impracticable. Nevertheless, when the Sovereign Pontiff, contrary to all expectation, decreed the re-establishment of the Mission, was it not, in reality, the voice of Jesus Christ Himself, declaring by his Vicar, " He that is to come, will come, and will not delay ?" (Hebrews x. 37.)

Meanwhile the Missioners took up their station provisionally in the great island of Lew Chew, situated at the gates of Japan, and inhabited by a population Japanese in origin, manners and language : " This island," adds Mgr. Forcade, " is a sort of outpost for us." Several years passed away before the Missioners were able to enter Japan. Mgr. Forcade had the consolation of converting and baptizing, in 1850, the Japanese who had taught him the language. Two years later he was obliged, by declining health, to return to France, and the Rev. Mr. Libois, the Procurator-General for Foreign Missions at Hong-Kong, found himself charged with the care of the Mission.

Further measures were taken in the course of the year 1853. The Rev. Mr. Collin, a Missioner in Mandchooria, was named Prefect-Apostolic of Japan. He was preparing to obey the mandate of the Sovereign Pontiff, when death struck him rather suddenly in the arms of Bishop Verrolles, on the 23d of May,

1854. The Rev. Mr. Libois, Provisional-Superior of the Mission, sent the Rev. Messrs. Girard, Mermet and Furet to Lew Chew. A first voyage, undertaken by the Rev. Mr. Furet, on the coast of Japan, was unproductive of any result. In the month of May of the following year (1856), the same Missioner and the Rev. Mr. Mounicou, both attached as interpreters to two French frigates, undertook a second voyage to the northern part of the archipelago. At Hakodadi (island of Yeso), they made several excursions on land, but the police followed them wherever they went, to prevent the natives holding communication with them. This watch was, however, baffled by the subaltern officers themselves, who took advantage of every moment they were safe from the vigilance of their superiors, to exchange a few words with the strangers who understood and spoke their language. Generally the people seemed well disposed, but were under the influence of fear. Similar dispositions were perceived by the Rev. Mr. Furet in one of the southern islands. The two Missioners were obliged, with regret, to return to Nafa (Lew Chew), to await, in prayer, study, and resignation, a more favorable opportunity.

The happy moment was not long delayed. Actuated, as it appeared, by merely commercial interest, but, in reality, obeying the dictates of Providence, Japan broke through its haughty isolation. Since the year 1854, signalized by some concessions granted to the Dutch, the government of Yedo has entered successively into commercial relations with the

United States of America, England, and Russia. In 1858 came the turn of France. The embassy, which was to conclude the first treaty of Tien-Tsing, arrived at Yedo on the 25th September. One of the Missioners of Lew Chew, the Rev. Mr. Mermet, acted as interpreter to the Baron Gros, minister plenipotentiary. The 9th of September following, the treaty was signed. By its provisions the three ports of Yokohama, Nagasaki, and Hakodadi were opened to French traders, and liberty of worship was granted to the foreign residents. This did not ensure entire liberty, since the priest was not able to exercise his ministry, except in the case of foreigners; but even half toleration was looked upon as affording an opening to a much better state of things. The Rev. Mr. Gerard, then recently appointed Pro-Vicar-Apostolic of Japan, wrote from Hong Kong to the Central Councils of the Society for the Propagation of the Faith (November 28, 1858): "After ten years of expectation and painful uncertainty regarding the fate of a Mission always especially dear to us, to see its gates opening themselves to us, is an event evidently due to the direct intervention of Providence. By a provision of the treaty, the plenipotentiary has a right to travel throughout the empire. Our hope is, that one of us may be able to accompany him, and seek out the remnants of the ancient flocks which must still exist in Japan. One of the European plenipotentiaries has told the Rev. Mr. Libois, that he has heard from the Japanese interpreters that there are Christians living in the mountains, and that many of them have lately been put to death on account of their faith."

The recent persecution here alluded to by the Rev. Mr. Girard, broke out in 1856 in the environs of Nagasaki. A Christian, living in a village which was the scene of the persecution, has since given the following details to the Missioners: "At least eighty Christians were arrested. Their relatives and friends went in crowds to the palace of the governor of Nagasaki, thinking that the prisoners would be restored to them. In fact, a great number were given up, but some thirty remained prisoners. What happened in the prison? Ten of them died within its walls. The rest being set at liberty a year or two after, nearly all died at home in consequence of the bad treatment to which they had been subjected. They were made to suffer in succession hunger, thirst, flogging, dislocation of the limbs. Their nails were torn off, and, at last, they were almost crushed to death under the weight of enormous stones. The bodies of those who had expired in prison were thrown into the place in which criminals were buried; but at night, the Christians collected their remains, and gave them honorable buria .

The treaty of 1858 inaugurated a new era in the history of the Church of Japan. The Missioners at once began to take active measures. The Rev. Mr. Girard accompanied to Yedo Mr. Duchéne de Bellecourt, consul-general of France, and was presented by him to the local authorities as interpreter and Catholic Priest. In his double capacity of interpreter to the consulate and head of the Mission, he was obliged to repair alternately to Yedo and Yokohama, a small town, only a few miles from the capital. He had with him at Yokohama one of his brother Priests, the Rev. Mr. Mounicou. The two Missioners built a chapel, which they solemnly blessed on the 12th January, 1861, in the midst of a numerous assembly of residents of all countries and creeds.

This was the first Catholic Church opened in Japan for more than two centuries; consequently, it became an object of interest to curious visitors, and the Japanese resorted thither, not only from Yokohama, Kanagaoura, Yedo, and the environs, but even from the farthest provinces. "These visits," wrote the Rev. Mr. Girard, "were no doubt due, in the first instance, to curiosity; nevertheless, they supplied us with an occasion of announcing Jesus Christ and his Gospel to a multitude of people, who listened to us with the greatest interest. For the last month the church has never been empty from morning till night, and each day we explain, with the aid of the pictures which adorn it, the abridgment of our holy religion to hundreds of persons. We have been told that our church had, in the beginning, so struck the Japanese, that a drawing of it had appeared in the capital, from which several copies were taken."

The government being alarmed at this concourse of its subjects, published a severe prohibition against their visiting the chapel. "The police keep a sharp look out on us," wrote the Rev. Mr. Mounicou (December 6th, 1861), "watching our every step. Our servants are taken from us after they have been a few months in our service, and we learn, from a trustworthy source, that two persons have been sent to the prisons of Yedo for having sold us two books without special authorization from their masters."

There were still to be seen at Yedo, and in the surrounding country, stone columns, on which were inscribed the penal edicts; the cross was represented on them, and underneath was written a death-warrant against whomsoever should pay the least marks of respect to that symbol.

The Japanese embassy having visited the countries of Europe in 1862, hopes were raised in consequence that Japan would henceforth grant free admission to the Catholic Missioners and Christian civilization. But th's hope was soon extinguished. Emboldened by the concessions granted by the courts of Europe to their ambassadors, the government of Yedo appeared disposed to maintain, with more tenacity than ever, their policy of exclusion. "They say," observed one of the Missioners, "that the authorities are sorry for having concluded the treaties, and that they would like to send away the strangers, or, at least, confine them to the ports open to traders as had formerly been done with the Dutch in the islet of Desima. In order to compass this end, they never ceased demanding one concession after another from the representatives of foreign nations, while the condescension which they too often met with rendered them every day more and more exacting." "Would you believe it," observed another Missioner, "that the governor of Yokohama has requested Mr. Dury, our consul, to have the three Chinese characters, inscribed on the front of our chapel removed, under the pretence that the Europeans, for whom it was built, do not read Chinese? Our ministry would not be unfruitful, were it not that an iron arm restrains the tendency of the multitude to embrace the truth. The people thirst for the truth all the more ardently, because the innumerable sects here leave them in dire uncertainty concerning the dogmatic questions it is most important for man to know. In the sea of errors which surrounds them, the Japanese seize with eagerness the plank of salvation when they catch a glimpse of it. If they had only their liberty, they would be converted by thousands." "The Japanese," wrote, on his side, the Rev. Mr. Girard, "long for the day when, better informed of our object and the benefits we bring with us, the government will no longer force its subjects to keep away from us by terrible threats. 'When,' say they, 'the present difficulties are removed, and relations between our country and foreign governments are established on more solid bases, we will ask France to send us a great number of the masters whose instruction we have already received; we wish to adore the God they worship, and to do so in the way they will teach us.'" Notwithstanding the prohibition concerning the church of Yokohama, many of the Japanese continued to visit it.

There were no grounds for hoping that complete religious toleration would be gained; but trusting in Him who is master of all events, the Missioners prepared the way for future and much-desired occasions. The oratory of Nagasaki was insufficient for its purpose, and they entertained the project of replacing it by a church. Thanks to an offering from the empress of the French and a subscription got up among the foreign residents, the works were begun in 1863. A handsome donation from Admiral Jaurès, and the fees for a French class at the Japanese college, helped the Rev. Messrs. Furet and Petitjean to meet all expenses; and, in less than two years, the church of St. Peter Baptist and his Companions was finished. Elsewhere we have related the circumstances attending the completion and blessing of the new church. "This church," wrote the Rev. Mr. Petitjean, "excited general admiration. The gilt crosses of its three steeples glitter within sight of Nagasaki. Old folks and young, men and women, soldiers and civilians, make it a party of pleasure to come and see the French church as they call it. The children of the city make drawings of it in charcoal on the walls and on the pavement of the public road. The old people recall the history of the past in regard to the Christians and their temples. I was informed lately of the site of the former churches of Nagasaki. In the course of a pilgrimage which we made to the holy mountain some years since, a pagan told us that a pagoda, which we had just passed, was formerly a Christian temple."

The new church of Nagasaki attracted an extraordinary concourse of visitors, but the Missioners were far, indeed, from thinking that it should be the means used by Providence for discovering the Japanese congregations. This important fact requires to be related with some details.

The first Christians who made themselves known belonged to a village not far from the city, and inhabited by thirteen hundred of the faithful. This took place on Friday, the 17th March, 1865. We must here allow one of the Missioners, namely, the Rev. Mr. Petitjean, to relate what follows: " About half-past twelve o'clock, some fifteen persons came to the door of the church. Directed no doubt by my good angel, I went up to them and opened the door. I had hardly time to recite a *Pater* when three women, from fifty to sixty years of age, knelt down beside me, and said to me in a low tone, laying their hands on their breasts: 'In our hearts, all we who are present are the same as you.' 'Can that be possible?' Where, then, do you come from?' They mentioned their village, and added: 'At home, nearly every one thinks as we do.' Praise be to Thy name, O Lord, for the joy that filled my soul at that moment. What a compensation that was for five years' sterile ministry! Hardly had the poor Japanese discovered themselves to me, when they became confidential in a way that contrasted strangely with the habits of their pagan countrymen. I had to satisfy all their questions, and speak to them of *O Deous Sama, O Yaso Sama, Santa Maria Sama*, names by which they designated God, our Lord Jesus Christ, and the Blessed Virgin.[1] The sight of Our Lady with the Infant Jesus reminded them of the festival of Christmas, which they celebrated in the eleventh month, they told me. They asked me were we not now at the seventeenth day of the mournful season (Lent). Neither was St. Joseph unknown to them; they called him the adopted father of Our Lord: *O Yaso Samano yo fou.* While questions were being asked me on all sides, the sound of approaching footsteps was heard. There was a general dispersion at once. But the moment the newcomers were descried, all returned laughing at the fright they had been in. 'These are people of our own village. They are of the same mind as ourselves.' However, we had in the end to separate, lest suspicion might be excited on the part of the officers, whose visit I dreaded."

On Holy Thursday and Good Friday, the 13th and 14th of April, fifteen hundred persons visited the church of Nagasaki; the Missioners' dwelling was literally invaded; the Christians took advantage of the opportunity to satisfy their devotion in secret before the crucifixes and statues of the Blessed Virgin. In the early days of May, the Missioners heard of the existence of two thousand five hundred Christians dispersed in the country round Nagasaki. On the 10th, the Christians flocked in such numbers that, to avoid the danger of being recognized by the satellites, the church had to be closed during a part of the day.

---

[1] In Japanese the word *sama* signifies king, sovereign.

"On the 15th of May," wrote the Rev. Mr. Petitjean, "deputies arrived from an island not far distant. After a short interview we sent them away, detaining only the catechist and the chief of the pious caravan. The catechist, whose name was Peter, gave us the most valuable information. In the first place, we may remark that his form of baptism differs in no respect from ours, and that he pronounced it very distinctly. There are still, he assured us, a great number of Christians in Japan, a few in every part. One district he particularly indicated, in which are grouped together more than a thousand families. He wished to hear from us about the Great Chief of the kingdom of Rome. When we assured him that the august Vicar of Jesus Christ, the saintly Pius IX, would be very happy to hear the consoling intelligence that he and his Christian countrymen had just given us, Peter's delight was unbounded; and yet, for all that, he was careful before leaving us to satisfy himself that we really were the successors of the old Missioners. 'Have you no children?' he timidly inquired. 'You, and all your Christians and pagan countrymen, are the children the good God has given us. As for other children, we cannot have any; the Priests, like your ancient Missioners, keep celibacy all their life.' On receiving this answer, Peter and his companion, bending their foreheads to the ground, exclaimed, 'They are virgins. Thanks! thanks!'"

Next day, an entire Christian village came to visit the Missioners, and two days later, six hundred other Christians sent to Nagasaki a deputation of twenty persons. On the 8th of June, twenty Christian congregations were known to the Missioners, and seven baptizers were placed in direct relation with them. "Our flock in distant districts," wrote the Rev. Mr. Petitjean, "throw us into despondency, and overwhelm us with joy at the same time, by their too great number and their filial dependence. Some of them come from twenty to thirty leagues, in boats or on foot, to visit the church, have an interview with us, and ask for crosses and medals. We continue, as often as possible, our nocturnal reunions. Our Lord has disciples even in Nagasaki." And on the 11th of June, we find the following entry in the journal of the Mission: "Visit during the night of three baptizers, who have all preserved the sacramental form unaltered. They tell us that, in their town and the neighboring one, there are seven or eight thousand Christians. The three visitors are well instructed. One of them begged us to give him a rosary, and then asked for a discipline to scourge himself when he prays God to pardon him his sins."

Day after day deputations continued to succeed one another. The police began to be on the alert, and the Japanese were forbidden to visit the church. However, the results of the prohibition were not so grievous as might have been apprehended.

Some extracts from the journal of the Rev. Mr. Petitjean will still farther show the relations established between the Christians and the Missioners:

"31st July, 1865.—A catechist presented himself at noon-day to make inquiries concerning the accuracy of the prayers contained in a book which some weeks before he had placed in my hands. He likewise brought me another for examination. With the exception of some faults of pronunciation and mistakes in copying, these prayers are a literal translation of the Sign of the Cross, the Lord's Prayer, the Angelical Salutation, the Apostles' Creed, the *Confiteor*, the Act of Contrition, Meditations on the Mysteries of the Rosary, etc.

"16th August.—Peter, the baptizer, the same who first revealed to us the devotion of our Christians for the Rosary, came to us at night with two companions. They wanted to get instruction on the manner of assisting the dying, and they gave us details of numerous congregations, whose existence was quite unknown to us.

"30th August.—Clara and Marina, each the mother of a family, whom we had already seen in the church, told us, after having assisted at Mass, that the inhabitants of their hamlet would be happy to receive the visits of the Missioners on the feast of one of their patron saints. The Feast of St. Clare, the first patron of the hamlet, being past, they would wish to have us on the Feast of St. Thecla. I observed to them that it would be difficult for us just at present to comply with their desire, on account of the danger to which we should expose the faithful. Formerly, there was in this village a fine church, under the invocation of St. Clare, some vestiges of which remain to the present day.

"During the night of the same day a catechist

brought us a man whom he was teaching to be a baptizer. They each asked us for beads, crucifixes, and pictures of St. Michael. It may be mentioned that, out of every ten Christians, five bear the name of Mighéron (Michael), and that St. Michael is universally regarded as one of the patrons of the empire.

"Many of our Christians preserve among them, with religious veneration, in order to transmit them to their descendants as they had received them from their forefathers, statues, pictures of Our Lord, the Blessed Virgin, and the Saints. We are convinced that these objects of devotion have greatly contributed to perpetuate among them the spirit of faith and the practice of the Christian virtues.

"September 17th.—During the last fifteen days we have received several visits from our Christians. Some of them came from a distance of forty or fifty leagues."

About the same time, the Missioners received a well-authenticated account of a village, the entire population of which, amounting to two thousand, profess Christianity. Wonderful to relate, they had an almost perfect knowledge of our mysteries, of the decalogue and sacraments, of prayer, the honor paid to the Blessed Virgin, the Angels and Saints. They led a life of penance, making frequent acts of contrition, especially at the hour of death. There was not a single book in the entire village, and yet the inhabitants, for the most part, knew by heart the Lord's Prayer, the Angelic Salutation, the Apostles' Creed, the *Confiteor*, the *Salve Regina*, etc. Several recited a treatise on contrition. One family possessed a picture representing the fifteen Mysteries of the Rosary. The people of the village and vicinity were in the habit of coming to venerate this picture, which they believed to have belonged to the first Missioners.

We may pause here to remark the care which the first apostles of Japan, and their immediate successors, took on the approach of the Dutch Protestants, to inculcate on the minds of the faithful the three points of Catholic teaching most opposed to the new errors: the primacy of the Holy See, the celibacy of the clergy, and the honor paid to the Blessed Virgin. These were, in fact, the first three points about which they questioned the Missioners, and the signs by which the Japanese Christians recognized them as their lawful pastors.

"I have been told by the chiefs of the same parish," wrote the Rev. Mr. Petitjean, "that in their village, and a good many others, there has been no trampling on the cross for a long time. This exemption is due to the local princes, who are not sorry in this way to show they can act independently of the court of Yedo. The same individuals have, moreover, told me that the Christian officers often substituted pictures of the god Schaka for those of Jesus Christ and His holy Mother, that the people might trample on them when that revolting practice was in vogue; a practice happily abolished altogether since the arrival of the Europeans in Japan.

"Among the numerous questions I have been required to answer, I may particularize the following: 'Your kingdom and that of Rome, are they of the one mind?' 'Have you been sent by the great chief of the kingdom of Rome?' 'Will others soon come to join you?' On receiving answers in the affirmative, they seemed greatly pleased. They were most anxious to know the Holy Father's name and his age. Also they wished to know who had come to our aid, and enabled us to build the fine church at Nagasaki. This gave me an opportunity of telling them of the Work of the Propagation of the Faith. 'But why,' they would ask me, 'will you not receive our poor offerings, when you accept those of your friends in other countries?' Prudence generally makes us refuse their gifts, lest we might furnish the government with a pretext for dealing harshly with us or with them. Having explained our motive, they appeared to be satisfied. I added, that if, in time to come, we should want money to build chapels and undertake other works, we would take advantage of their good will."

In spite of the prudence of the Missioners in their communications with the congregations so wondrously discovered, the newspapers, owing to an indiscretion which it is needless to dwell upon, got wind of the discovery and published the news, without, however, giving details or commentaries. Now, the Rev. Mr. Petitjean wrote afterwards as follows, January 29, 1866: "The half-publicity given to our discoveries by the European press, obliges us to strict silence. To avoid exciting the hostility of the government, we make ourselves as insignificant as we can, meet our catechists as seldom as possible, and refrain from doing anything calculated to compromise the Mission."

In the course of the year 1866, two incidents put the Missioners of Nagasaki on their guard. A boat, on board which were a number of Christians, was stopped; the latter were sent to prison, so as to force them to discover the name of their village. Some time after, a Japanese officer summoned before him the chiefs of another Christian village, and advised them not to go " to the European *bonzery*," lest they might get themselves into great trouble. These incidents served for a warning, and indicated the possibility of an approaching persecution. The Christians, however, were no way affected; even the children asked to receive confirmation, that they might be strengthened to confess the Faith.

Meanwhile, a new pledge of hope was vouchsafed to the Church of Japan. The Holy Father appointed as Vicar-Apostolic the Rev. Mr. Petitjean, who was consecrated at Hong-Kong on the 21st October, 1866, by Mgr. Guillemin, Prefect-Apostolic of Kouang-Tong.

. On the 26th December following, the new Bishop wrote : " The number of our flock preparing for communion daily increases. In fact, up to this, we have thought it well to try the fidelity of our Christians by delaying their admission to the Holy Table. The apostolic zeal of our catechists is more than ever actively manifested. One of them is about to turn hawker for the purpose of discovering such Christians as have not yet shown themselves. He will be accompanied by a pagan friend, who is anxiously asking to be baptized."

"On the 4th and 6th February," we read in another letter from Bishop Petitjean, "we confirmed during the night more than eighty Christians, who had been preparing for the sacrament since Christmas. They had, at the same time, the happiness of receiving their First Communion."

III.

Up to that time, notwithstanding that some apprehensions were excited, the peace of the Mission remained undisturbed. It was the will of God, no doubt, that the revivified Church should have its faith strengthened before new trials assailed it.

The Missioners, in fact, foresaw that the day would come, when, on the refusal of the Christians to receive the ministry of the bonzes at the funerals of their relatives, the mandarins would certainly interfere. The day came at last. One of the Christians having died, his relatives came in all haste to the Missioners, to know whether they could allow the bonze to perform the usual ceremonies over the body of the departed. As soon as the doctrine of the Church was explained to them, they gave notice of the death to the choya or civil magistrate, without troubling themselves about the bonzes. The latter denounced the Christians at once as infringers of the law, and the choya threatened to bring the affair under the notice of the governor of Nagasaki. The situation of affairs became complicated by the occurrence of another death, as we shall see by extracts from the correspondence of the Rev. Mr. Armbruster, Missioner at Nagasaki.

"16th April, 1867.—A deputation came to us from Ourakami. A Christian woman had just died. The choya having been informed of the fact, gave a ticket for the bonze, but the relatives said they did not require the services of that functionary. The choya insisted, threatened to denounce them to the government, referred to the last persecution, and the possibility of its recurrence, and advised them to consider the matter. Our good Christians did not hesitate a moment between the fear of persecution and the sense of duty; they did what was right, even at the risk of their life.

"17th April.—Another deputation. Several Christian villages of the valley assembled under the presidency of their mayors, and came to the resolution of sending a deputation to the choya. The deputies are to declare that they are faithful subjects of the Japanese government, that they will always be found obedient to the officers of the State, but that they strongly desire to have no communication whatever with the bonzes.

"18th April.—The choya gave a favorable reception to the deputation, expressing at the same time his apprehensions, and the serious pain the affair caused him. The deputies understood that the choya was afraid of losing his situation. Actuated by a feeling of the noblest charity, they made him the following reply: 'We greatly regret the annoyance you feel on the occasion, but do not be uneasy. If, on our account, you lose your place, we pledge ourselves that we will continue to pay your annual salary.' The magistrate was touched by such a proposal. 'Give me,' he said, 'a list of all the families who do not want to have any thing to do with the bonzes, and I will present it myself to the governor.' Then turning the conversation on religious matters, he gave expression to his esteem for a doctrine which was capable of inspiring such generous sentiments.

"On all sides, the Christian families got their names inscribed on the lists. At St. Clare, there were more than one hundred; at St. Francis Xavier, more than two hundred. One thing was certain, namely, that henceforth the choya, and through him the governor of Nagasaki, would be aware of our relations with the Christians.

"One of the sons of the deceased woman of Ourakami has informed the bishop that he and his brother-in-law have been summoned before the daicouan (prefect of police), at Nagasaki. What will be the consequence of this? 'I expect,' he continued, 'to be put in prison, and perhaps beheaded, but I don't care.' Certainly this Christian and his brother-in-law, quiet, humble, God-fearing men, have shown great courage. The choya advised them to go accompanied by some deputies from the village, and to take advantage of the circumstance to ask the daicouan for the permission they desired. The inhabitants of the village vied with one another for the honor of accompanying them.

"20th April.--The deputies and the sons of the departed received Holy Communion at two o'clock in the morning. Afterwards they repaired to the house of the daicouan; the choya of the valley, his principal officers, and the mayor of the village escorted them. According to the Japanese custom, the deputies were all old men. One of our most zealous catechists, Dominic, fearing that they might be intimidated, managed to be sent with them. The deputies were twenty in number; the choya would not venture to introduce more than five to the daicouan; Dominic was among the number. About eight o'clock in the evening, Dominic came to tell us what had taken place: 'Early in the morning,' he reported, 'we were brought to the daicouan's court; but the examination did not take place till noon. The daicouan, accompanied by all his officers, then entered the hall. Addressing, in the first instance, the sons of the departed, he said: 'You have buried your mother without giving notice to the choya or the bonze.' 'I informed the choya,' replied one of them, 'but it is quite true I did not send word to the bonze.' 'And what was your motive for not calling in the bonze? You know the law, of course.' I then undertook to speak: 'We do not like the bonzes; and this feeling we inherit from our ancestors.' 'Why do you not like them?' 'We do not believe in their doctrine.' 'But for all that, you must conform to the customs of Japan, and call in the bonzes.' 'We are the emperor's subjects, disposed to obey him in all things. Our way obliges us, even as a duty, to do so.' But we cannot call in the bonzes; it is contrary to our way, and you could not oblige us to do so. 'What, then, is the way that you follow?' 'The way we have learnt from our ancestors; it makes us content in this life, and secures us perfect happiness in the next.' The daicouan listened with interest to my replies, and asked for explanations of the Christian doctrine. I excused myself, while at the same time answering a great number of questions. At last I said to him: 'I am only a poor laboring man, and know no more than is necessary for me to know. But have the goodness to go to our masters the French Priests: they will explain to you the way we follow; it is the same that they teach, and that we have inherited from our ancestors.'

"An officer took down all my answers. The daicouan showed us marked kindness throughout; in conclusion, he said the matter should be submitted to the governors. We then left; but as soon as the governors had arrived, we were summoned again. The first governor asked the accused, 'why he had buried his mother without complying with the legal formalities?' He gave the same answer he had given the daicouan. The governor was angry. 'The emperor requires you to call in the bonzes,' he said, 'and

---

[1] In Japan the word *way* means religion, doctrine; thus, *sintoism*, or religion of spirits, literally signifies *way* of spirits (Sin-to); the doctrine of Confucius means *way* of letters (Syou-to).

conform to their way. You are only poor laborers, and ought to think of nothing but tilling your ground, taking care of your relatives, bringing up your family, and minding your health.'

"The old men, deeply affected, maintained a profound silence. I ventured to say: 'We do not call in the bonzes because we do not believe in them.' 'What! you are the youngest, and you dare to speak when the old men keep silent!' The governor began to use harsh language. I made signs to the old men to speak; but they were so upset that they could not say a word. One alone among them gave tokens that he approved what I was saying. At last the governor dismissed us with these words: 'Well, then, what is it you want?' 'One thing only we want,' I replied, 'and that is, not to be constrained to call in the bonzes or enter the pagodas.' 'Is not every one at liberty in Japan,' returned the governor, 'to go into the pagodas or to stay away?'

"When we had left, the choya said to the old men: 'Why did you say nothing? You ought to have spoken like your comrade. Come to-morrow, and I will let you know the governor's answer.'

"Such was Dominic's account. Ten years ago, matters would not have turned out exactly in that way. Our courageous catechist would have been well tortured in punishment for his daring answers. However, the affair is not over yet; the difficulty is as great as ever. We finished the day by solemnly baptizing twenty-three adults.

"22d April.—Yesterday evening, the choya of Onrakami gave audience to the deputies of the city. He told them that it is the governor's wish that they should call in the bonzes for their interments, in conformity with the custom of the empire. He told them not to lose courage, to present themselves again before the governor, and petition him to dispense them from usages contrary to the way they had embraced. Nay, he even promised to go with them and support them in their application.

"23d April.—At night-fall, twenty-five neophytes of Ourakami received baptism.

"24th April.—The Vicar-Apostolic received a visit from a Christian woman, who came from a great distance, though she is seventy-two years of age. The village she lives in has a population of about three hundred families, all of whom are Christians. We hear that the choya of Ourakami hast just sent to the governor of Nagasaki the lists of the families who petitioned to be delivered from the yoke of the bonzes.

"28th April.—A person has just died at Oùrakami. The choya has been informed. Here we meet again the great difficulty. The affair has been referred to the governor, who has dispensed with the attendance of the bonze. The rumor of what the Christians had done reached the city. Dominic brought the bishop a list of fifty pagans in Nagasaki anxious to embrace our religion and to study the Christian doctrine. At Ourakami several pagans have had themselves enrolled among the catechumens.

"29th April.—An inhabitant of a neighboring village says that the choya of that quarter has threatened to send into banishment all who hold any communication with us. The officers of Omoura, who reside at Ourakami, forbid the Japanese of their government to have anything to say to us. In spite of the prohibition, children are brought to us every night from the province of Omoura, that they may be baptized."

The months of May and June passed by without any remarkable danger in the situation of affairs. From the 1st January, 1867, to the 9th June, the number of first communions had increased to about twelve hundred. In a letter, written the 14th June, to the Directors of the Seminary for Foreign Missions, the Rev. J. Cousin gives the following description of a religious ceremony which took place at Nagasaki some days previously. The 2d June will be a memorable day in the history of our Mission. I allude to the inauguration of the statue of the Blessed Virgin, which, at the request of our Bishop, you sent to Nagasaki. The French minister and Admiral Roze, who had lately arrived on board the frigate *Guerrière*, were good enough to accept Mgr. Petitjean's invitation, and promised to assist at the ceremonies.

"Every one lent a hand to the work. While the Japanese prepared garlands of leaves and flowers, our brave seamen pitched, opposite the church, a tent to shelter the statue of Mary and the altar on which the Holy Sacrifice will be celebrated. In the centre of the most elevated plot a pedestal was raised, destined to receive *Our Lady of Japan*. She will be there, within view of all, as a memorial of the victory gained over the demon, whose images were hitherto the only ones allowed to be seen in public. 'What recollections and what hopes are associated with this title of Our Lady of Japan!' observed the French minister, whose great mind comprehended all the significance of the manifestation. And, truly, neither God nor His Holy Mother will forget the inscription on the pedestal of the statue: *Our Lady of Japan, pray for us! In memoriam diei 17 Martii, 1865.*[1] On the right and left of this inscription, the following touching and appropriate invocations are inscribed: *Regina martyrum. Auxilium Christianorum.*

"The approach to the church of Nagasaki is by a flight of steps, along which are parterres ornamented with flowers. On each side of the altar erected on that occasion under the porch of the church, praying desks and seats were placed for the French minister and the foreign consuls, the admiral and his staff. Lower down, nearer the statue, and on the upper gallery of our habitation, the European residents and the band of the frigate were stationed: lastly, the Japanese, in great numbers, filled the garden and the space about the church.

"Striking, indeed, was the scene when our prelate, clothed in his pontifical vestments, and surrounded by his five Missioners, ascended the altar. However, there was more in it than a merely beautiful sight.

---

[1] In memory of the 17th March, 1865. (The day on which the Japanese congregations were discovered.)

From the altar, which commands the prospect, the port, so lately closed against strangers, is seen below; to the right is the city where, formerly, instruments of torture were prepared for our twenty-six martyrs; and, farther on, rises the mountain on which were immolated these invincible witnesses of Jesus Christ. In fine, it is Japan, the land in which the cross was trampled under foot. And now the day has come when France, represented in a threefold manner, in her religious strength, civilizing influence and warlike power, by a bishop, a minister plenipotentiary, and an admiral, kneeling together before the same God, publicly takes her part in the sacrifice of the cross, and raises a monument to the Queen of Heaven, whom she proclaims Our Lady of Japan! Surely, considered from this point of view, the ceremony was a real triumph.

"This triumph was indicated in a few words which fell from the lips of the Vicar-Apostolic at the beginning of the ceremony. 'Our Lady of Japan,' said the prelate, 'is not a new title given to the Blessed Virgin. From the beginning the Mission has been under her patronage, and Mary has shown that she has watched over her charge with unfailing solicitude. And so, when the Sovereign Pontiff confided to us the difficult office and the honor of representing him in these distant regions, our first thought was to consecrate to this good Mother our own person and the Church she has preserved from total destruction. This festivity is, therefore, an offering of thanksgiving; moreover, it will be a pledge of protection for the nations who are so nobly represented. In thee, then, Our Lady of Japan, we place all our hopes!'

"After Mass, the official report of the ceremony was signed by those present, and deposited in the interior of the statue of Our Lady, who has thus been constituted guardian of the land. The illumination of the façade of the Church and of the ornamental plots serving as an avenue to the edifice, brought the ceremony to a conclusion. The French and Portuguese consuls generously contributed to defray the expenses. In spite of the rain, which had been threatening us during the previous three days, the illumination succeeded admirably. The vice-governor of the city, accompanied by the French consul, approached to the very foot of the statue of Mary, and offered his congratulations to the bishop."

At the very time that the practice of honoring the Mother of God was restored after an interval of two centuries in Japan, the Church was preparing a triumph for the ancestors of the new Christians. On the 7th of July, the pontifical decree was published at Rome, declaring Blessed two hundred and five of the innumerable Confessors put to death in the seventeenth century.[1] If the persecutions, which recommenced some days after the celebration of Nagasaki and Rome, have not had the same character as the

---

[1] These two hundred and five martyrs, chosen from those who suffered from the 22d May, 1617, to the 3d September, 1632, represent all classes of civil society, and all the religious Orders engaged in evangelizing Japan up to that time, the Franciscans, Dominicans, Jesuits, and Augustinians.

preceding, may we not attribute this advantage to the twofold mediation of the Blessed Virgin and the holy Martyrs?

During the night of the 14-15th July, 1867, some officers, followed by a number of satellites, arrested at Ourakami about sixty Christians, irrespective of age or sex, bound and ill-used them, and led them away to prison. The following letter was written by the Rev. J. Laucaigne to the Directors of the Seminary for Foreign Missions:

"Nagasaki, 18th July, 1867.—A courier brings us intelligence of the arrest of several of the principal Christians, men and women, of Our Lady of the Epiphany, on Monday last, at three o'clock in the morning. There was a report that the son of the baptizer was flogged to such a degree that he was left half dead. The chapel was pillaged and ransacked.

"Francis Xavier, one of our catechists, was returning from Mass when news of the disaster reached Nagasaki. He crossed the sea at once, and arrived in the valley just as the prisoners were being led away to the city. From him I had the most particular account of the sad events of the morning. First of all, he told me of the arrest of his father (the mayor of·the village of St. Francis Xavier), and the barbarous way he was treated by the satellites, who beat him with sticks and bound him, not giving him time to take his clothes. Though merely a catechumen, he has shown great patience and courage. The executioners were astonished, and said to one another: 'This is a true Christian indeed; you may beat him as long as you please, he never complains.' The eldest brother of Francis Xavier, a whole family of relatives, some young catechists, several women who came out to bid them farewell, the eldest brother of another catechist, a young girl who occupied herself in instructing her companions, and a woman with her child, aged two years, complete the list of those who were put in bondage for the name of Jesus Christ. On leaving the village of St. Francis, the troop of persecutors, amounting to about three hundred men, divided into parties, and fell simultaneously on the villages of St. Clare, St. Joseph and Our Lady of the Epiphany. At St. Clare, the first Christian seized was an old man, who had been imprisoned during the late persecution. Having been recognized by one of the satellites, he was at once set at liberty. Less humanity was shown to a baptizer, whose father had suffered for the faith ten years ago; along with him were arrested and imprisoned one of his daughters, fifteen years of age, and several Christians from distant parts of the country, who had come to him to be instructed in the Christian doctrine.

"There was time, at St. Joseph of the Epiphany, to hide the different objects of devotion, while the satellites were occupied in arresting the baptizer and the two principal Christians. At Our Lady of the Epiphany, the satellites went at once to the proprietor of the site on which the chapel was built. When he heard the voices of the nocturnal visitors, and the continued knocking at the door, he thought of what had happened in 1856, when he was arrested with his father and mother. This time also, he hastily made his escape by a secret passage. While he was making for the woods, the chapel was given up to pillage. Without stopping to take the trouble of making a selection among the numerous Christians shut up in the chapel, the satellites arrested all who came in their way. 'Where is Mr. ——'s house, demanded an officer of the first young man he met. 'Here it is,' was the reply. 'And who are you?' 'I am the son of the person you are looking for.' Hearing this, the satellites stopped him, tied his hands behind his back, and pushed him on before them. The young man was in delicate health; the indignation of the old Christians was excited by the brutality with which he was treated, and the satellites got a few blows. Mr. ——, who is the baptizer of the village; his eldest son, another Christian, proprietor of a garden, which sometimes serves as a public walk for the European residents of Nagasaki, were bound and led along the road to the city.

"Immediately after their presentation to the choya, the Christians who had been arrested were put in prison. Of what occurred in the house of the choya, or in the prison, we know nothing. All we could learn was, that they practised a gross imposition on the Christians, and tried to make them appear as rebels. And this is the way they endeavored to compass their designs. The choya advised them to offer resistance to the satellites, and procure arms, promising his assistance and the help of his superior officers 'against whose will,' he said, 'these things had taken place.' I hastened to inform our dear prisoners of the stratagem, and to warn them against the new snare set for them, recommending them not to offer any resistance, no matter how badly they might be treated.

"The result of this day's work was the imprisonment of sixty-five, some say sixty-nine persons. The question is, are the arrests likely to go on? Our Christians, at any rate, are ready for whatever may happen, even if they should have to lay down their life. Let us hope that the Almighty will not require such a sacrifice."

Under date of the 27th July, the Vicar-Apostolic announced that the ministers of France and the United States interested themselves with the Japanese government in behalf of the incarcerated Christians. The following are extracts from the last letters of the Rev. Mr. Cousin:

"2d August.—The persecutors seem determined to continue their work. A Christian woman, named Clara, was brought up to-day before the criminal judge, to give an account of her conduct on the occasion of the recent death of her mother. Faithful to God and her conscience, she refused to call in the bonze, after giving notice to the civil officers. Being cited before the el oya and the daicouan, she protested that she never would have recourse to the bonze. The judge has just inquired whether she would not retract her first answers, and whether she persevered in her foolish obstinacy. On her reply, the executioners were ordered to put her in bonds.

"10th August.—We are now in possession of some details concerning the examination of Clara. The judge wished to save her, by making her say that it was through forgetfulness she neglected to call in the bonze. But she protested energetically that she acted designedly, to fulfil the last wishes of her mother, and to save her soul. Then it was that she was bound and cast into prison. She had said, when leaving the village, 'I shall never return; but I am not unhappy, for I can tell the other prisoners all that the Bishop and the Europeans are doing for us.'

"The mode of persecution adopted will become disastrous if persevered in. Many Christians, who now endure every kind of torture without shrinking, will, perhaps, find their courage fail at the thought that henceforth death will not strike a victim in their family without, by the same blow, sending other victims to pine away in dungeons.

"More deaths have occurred, and the number of the accused has been increased in consequence, summoned as they are even now to give an account of their conduct. Not long since, an old man came by night to receive the sacraments, so that he might next day fearlessly appear before the criminal judge.

"The Christians of Nagasaki are not the only sufferers. More than forty of our flock have lately been arrested in a neighboring province, namely, Omoura. The officers have taken a census, in which every one was to prove himself not to be a Christian by signing a declaration with his blood, drinking, at the same time, a draught of water, over which the bonzes had pronounced certain superstitious words. The inhabitants of the village of Coba, understanding that they were required to make an act of apostasy, refused to sign, declaring they would rather die than cease to be Christians. All, with the exception of women, and children under fifteen years of age, were thrown into prison. The Christians of the village of Kitamoura were, in the first instance, quite taken in; but subsequently discovering that an act of apostasy was required of them, they all went in a body protesting they were deceived, and that they were Christians like the people of Coba. Seven of their number were immediately incarcerated. The women and children asked to be allowed to share the same fate, but they were dismissed.

"Thus, many families are exposed to want and all manner of danger by the loss of their principal members. Our Christians of Ourakami, actuated by the dictates of their persecuted religion, and under an inspiration worthy of its sanctity, have gone in turn to keep watch over the desolate houses, uninhabited now save by widows and orphans.

"18th August.—My sad anticipations have been realized; in the two villages of Coba and Kitamoura there does not remain a single Christian; all, even the women and children are in prison; their desire has been thus accomplished. Communication with them is completely interrupted, so that it has become impossible to ascertain how they are treated, or to form an idea of the fate that awaits them. Unfavorable reports are afloat, to the effect that seven of them are destined to die, after which the rest will be set free. Nothing can be known for certain, except that the inferior officers urge the adoption of extreme measures, in the hope of deriving some profit from the executions. In the prisons of Omura are more than one hundred and ten confessors of the faith, and in those of Nagasaki more than sixty.

"Affairs seem to take a favorable turn at Nagasaki. The French minister will, it is said, obtain the immediate release of the prisoners and the restoration of their confiscated property. The governor of the city does not deny that he has received orders on the subject. We must, therefore, render thanks to God that He has shortened the time of trial. However, it must be acknowledged that neither our joy nor confidence can be at the present moment complete; our fear is that restrictive conditions will be imposed in the event of the liberation of the Christians."

In drawing our long account to a conclusion, we shall add some items of late news. The representatives of foreign powers take a lively interest in the fate of the Christians. To their influence, no doubt, may be attributed the fact that we have not to mourn over more numerous arrests. For example, one of their number, in an audience granted by the governor of Nagasaki, energetically combated the pretext put forward to justify the persecution.

"It is not in the name of treaties," said he to the

governor, "that I come here, but as a friend, and in the name of humanity, the laws of which you are violating. Europe will reprobate your proceedings; you will fall in her estimation once more into the ranks of barbarous nations, and your relations with her will suffer in consequence."

Two days later, another consul repeated the same argument to the governor; it is the only one capable of being understood or listened to.

Having heard of the destitution that had come upon certain families whose fathers were in prison, Mgr. Petitjean sent them some relief. They unanimously refused to accept assistance, saying that the Bishop and the Missioners had enough to do to provide or t e wants of those of whom they had taken charge.

"And, indeed, the fact is," writes the Rev. Mr. Cousin, "that the Bishop has gathered together, in a safe place, some orphans, especially those who have shown aptitude for Latin studies. So that the enemy of salvation, in depriving the Christian villages of the fathers of their families, has been instrumental in causing the foundation of a seminary, from which will issue forth, in time to come, his most formidable adversaries. Already twenty children have been collected; we have to make some sacrifices for their support, which we do not regret, but which will soon exhaust our resources, unless Divine Providence comes to our aid.

"Such of our Christians as have been admitted to the sacraments are strong in faith, and only for the express prohibition of the Bishop, would come in great numbers to confession every evening. I must tell you that two Christian women passed a whole night in the church waiting to receive the Holy Eucharist, and go back more courageous. One of them is married, and the mother or relative of several among the prisoners."

Such, on the 15th September, 1867, was the last news from Japan. The prayers of our Associates will bring these trials to a speedy conclusion. Certainly, they can only be temporary, for "it seems impossible," wrote one of the Missioners, "that God would have raised this Church from its ruins, only to let it fall into destruction again. Faith will surely triumph over these last efforts of the devil.'

LIFE OF THE

BLESSED CHARLES SPINOLA.

PART I.

PREPARATION FOR THE APOSTLESHIP.

I.—THE DESIRE OF BLESSED CHARLES FOR MARTYRDOM.

THE name of Spinola is famous in the military annals of Italy and the Low Countries.

In the sixteenth century Augustine Spinola distinguished himself by defending Genoa, his native city against the Gonzagas, and in many campaigns under Charles V. In the next age, Ambrose Spinola won still greater glory in defending Catholicity in Belgium. A great ornament was reserved for this family.

In 1564 there was born at Genoa a grandson of Augustine, who was to invest the name of Spinola with incomparable renown. This was Charles, son of Octavius Spinola, Count f Tassarolo, to whom the Sovereign Pontiff, Pius IX., has just decreed the martyr's palm.

Before describing the actions of the Blessed Charles, it will not be useless to show the principle which directed them. This principle was an immense desire of shedding his blood for Jesus Christ. In his eyes martyrdom was not only a crowning favor from heaven in reward for his devotedness, or an heroic act worthily closing a life consecrated to the glory of God; it was the object of his first aspirations, the aim of all his labors. Others like him have suffered for the diffusion of the Gospel, some even have been tortured with greater barbarity, in this point alone our hero has few equals: the thought of martyrdom governed his whole life, and inspired his most important resolutions. And as though God himself designed thus to teach us an important lesson, he has permitted us to know of the early youth of this illustrious martyr only this admirable disposition. The rest is either common to him and other members of his family, or is confined to vague indications: his inclination for martyrdom alone is noted.

This attraction came from heaven, as no one can doubt. But God took delight in the fidelity of his servant, as of old in Job's; he was pleased to contemplate in the child the heroic actions of his riper age, and he revealed them beforehand to his chosen souls. Thus, Father Bartholomew Ricci of the Society of Jesus learned the destiny of young Charles, and in the expansion of his joy, revealed to him the secret of God. These details we learn from the holy martyr's own lips. Towards the close of his life he recalled with emotion the wonderful dispositions of Divine Providence in his regard, and in the outpouring of a pious conversation he sometimes made known the graces that he had received. "I was still quite young," said he one day to a Japanese catechist, "and playing with other youths of my own age, when the Father who had charge of us during recreation took me apart, and told me that I would enter the Society of Jesus, and be sent to Japan to propagate the Faith. He foretold a third thing to me," he added, "but that is not yet verified."

The catechist's curiosity was strongly excited as to this mysterious point; but all his entreaty could obtain no light: he only learned that he should one day know. To a religious of his society, however, Father Spinola avowed that, according to the prediction, he was to have the happiness of shedding his blood for religion. Among the Japanese it was a generally received opinion that the holy missionary had from childhood known that God destined him for martyrdom.

Charles's education, without preparing him directly for the apostolic vocation, was nevertheless pious and careful, suited to the rank and traditions of his family. His education was that of a Spinola. When he had scarcely outgrown infancy he was taken to Spain, where several of his uncles held high positions. Returning to Italy he was confided to another uncle, Cardinal Philip Spinola, then administering the diocese of Nola. There living in the palace, and attending the college of the Society of Jesus, he resumed his scarcely commenced studies, and all the exercises of mind and body that were to fit him to follow a career worthy of his name. If he chose to enter the church, the Cardinal's favor opened the way to the highest dignities; if he preferred the splendors of the world, he might aspire to the most enviable posts, through the influence of his father, then Grand Equerry to the Emperor.

With such protection even mediocrity attains the foremost rank; what might not a nobleman expect who added to all these external advantages the most brilliant and solid personal qualities, and who sought to develop them by all the means afforded under the wise training of his teachers? Such were men's thoughts, and for a time Charles shared them, with this difference, that in a spirit of nobler ambition, he wished to owe everything to his own merit. Did he persist in these ideas after hearing the prediction of his apostleship and martyrdom? This is scarcely credible, if we consider the authority already enjoyed by Father Bartholomew Ricci, and the profound impression which the holy martyr retained to the end of his life, of this communication. God certainly claimed this great soul, now immersed in serious reflections. The brevity of this life, the uncertainty of the last hour, the instability of human affairs, the emptiness of honors that have no influence on eternity; on the other hand, the durability of the divine promises and what rests on them, the consolations of divine love, the sublimity of the Christian apostleship; these and other like considerations gradually weaned the young man from the world and disposed him for the most sublime designs. At the age of twenty, and just on the point of terminating his studies, Charles was in this happy state of mind when a great example of apostolic heroism gave him the decisive impulse.

Among the missionaries, who were continuing in the Indies the work of St. Francis Xavier, was Father Rudolph Aquaviva, an Italian like Charles, and of a family equally distinguished with the Spinolas. This worthy religious, after spending his strength in the service of the gospel, received the reward of his generosity: he was massacred by some islanders, in hatred of religion, July 15, 1583. When the tidings of his martyrdom reached Italy, Charles was deeply moved. To die for the faith, to shed his blood for Jesus Christ, seemed to him supreme happiness. Thenceforward all his thoughts tended to the means of attaining this end. His care in deciding on a choice of a state of life, the preference he gave to the Society of Jesus, his firm adherence to his vocation, his fervent practice of the duties of his profession; all are explained by his desire for martyrdom. Of this we have an authentic testimony in the letter which he wrote at a later day from his prison in Omura to the Very Rev. Father Mutius Vitelleschi, General of the Society of Jesus. After relating his arrest, as we shall see, he dwells complacently on the inappreciable favor, which the Almighty seems to reserve for him, that of dying for the faith. The humble religious dares not behold in this the just reward of his zeal; he attributes it to the prayers of Father Rudolph, "whose heroic death long since excited him to solicit with such earnestness his entrance into the Society and the Japanese mission."

II.—HIS VOCATION TO THE SOCIETY OF JESUS.

Impelled by his ardor for martyrdom, Charles had promptly decided to solicit admission into the Society of Jesus. The young candidate seemed to blend all desirable qualities, but prudence required his family's approval. Such was the reply of the superiors of the order. This condition was not easily fulfilled. Charles's parents were, indeed, too pious to reject absolutely all idea of a religious vocation, and they knew moreover that by formal opposition they would incur the anathema recently pronounced by the General Council of Trent; but on the other hand, had they not the right, were they not even bound to test their son's vocation? The principle is just, if certainty as to God's will alone is sought; but how often is it only a pretext for guilty plots! How many a child is diverted from his path and thrown into the most unbridled disorder, by the ambition or mistaken love of parents! The generous soul of Charles rebelled against human calculations; from the opposition of his kindred it drew new energy and additional motive for adhering to his design; but the consent of his family was not the less essential.

In an affair of this nature Charles correctly felt that his uncle's influence would always preponderate, and that by gaining him he would easily gain the rest. He accordingly wrote to him at Rome where he then was, employing in his letter all arguments to convince him. The uncle replied undecisively. New and more pressing letters from the nephew; new, kind, but always evasive replies from the uncle.

At last the Cardinal wrote that before deciding he must wait for the return of the Rector of Nola, then absent. Charles felt the danger of these prolonged delays, and in a moment of holy impatience replied by the following letter, inspired, one would say, by reading Saint Jerome :

I learn, on good authority, that the Father Rector will not return for some time : hence, unable to wait, I beg your Eminence to send me by return courier the permission I solicit, so as to be able to enter the Society on St. Thomas's day. For mercy's sake raise up no more delays, I can bear no more. We do not require the Rector, the Father Provincial is here to receive me. If your Eminence designed putting me off till I received a favorable reply from my father, you must know that in this I cannot depend on his approbation. Do what he will, he will not shake my resolution. I have even discussed this matter with your Eminence only from respect and courtesy, for I feel convinced that no permission is needed to carry out such designs. Hence, if I am so unhappy as not to obtain what I ask, I shall at last be compelled to exert the right which God gave me. I will go and shut myself up with the Fathers; they cannot repulse me, knowing that they owe more respect to God who calls me among them, than to men who wish to prevent my entrance. Were it otherwise, I should be bold enough to write to the Father General, and even, if needs be, make my petition reach the Sovereign Pontiff. Should all fail me, I can yet find some obscure nook, if at the end of the world, to live on roots and water: for if God is with me, who shall be against?

If in what I have just written I overstep the bounds of modesty, let your Eminence attribute it to the earnest desire that attracts me to the religious life. I trust that a Cardinal of Holy Church will not exert the authority vested in his august dignity to deprive of so great a blessing one who has the honor to be his nephew. After seconding the religious vocations of so many others, can you refuse to mine your favor and credit? Not to appear importunate, I insist no further.

Your Eminence's most humble and devoted
Servant,
CHARLES SPINOLA.

NOLA, December 7, 1584.

This warm letter produced the best effect on the clear mind and good heart of the Cardinal. Convinced that the young man's firmness came from God, he yielded, and immediately gave his approbation, influencing by his decision the consent of the whole family.

Great was Charles's joy at this intelligence, and so eager was he to profit by this disposition, that, ten days after, on the 23d of December, he entered the novitiate at Nola in the province of Naples.

III.—Fervor of the Young Novice.

The training of the novices at Nola was then confided to Father Bartholomew Ricci—the same one who had made known to young Charles the designs of Providence as to him. Imagine the joy and respect with which he welcomed the young novice! With what care he sought to correspond to the views of God. The care bestowed by St. Ignatius on St. Francis Xavier, must have been that of such a master for such a novice a truly paternal goodness, but no indulgence for natural inclinations; encouragement while exacting a strict practice of the most difficult virtues. Thus the master trained his disciple in humility, charity, obedience, the love of Jesus crucified; in a word, in all the virtues which specially dispose men for the apostolic life; and on his side the disciple devoted himself with a zeal worthy of the glorious death to which God had called him.

Without entering on the details of what constitutes the life of a fervent novice, we cannot omit one point on which, as Charles reasonably thought, depended the success of all his endeavors: his communings with God. To say that the pious novice faithfully discharged the duties of prayer, meditation and examination of conscience; in a word, all the exercises of piety prescribed by the rule, would be little; he went still further: he gave more time to prayer, always kneeling, immovable, and in the posture of a most humble suppliant. Two prayers (one at least of his own composition, and recited by him every morning), will give some idea of the fervor wherewith he was transported and the thoughts he entertained during these moments. We give them here for the edification of the reader :

I.

I adore Thee, most Holy Trinity, Father, Son, and Holy Spirit, my God and my all. I thank Thee for the gifts of creation, redemption and preservation; for the institution of the holy Sacraments, for my vocation to this Society; for the countless graces that Thou hast conferred upon me and for those Thou hast conferred upon all men. Behold me, Lord, all covered with the blood of thy divine Son! To Thy love, to Thy glory and to the salvation of my neighbor, I consecrate all that I am, all that is within or without me, the thoughts, words, actions of this day and of my whole life. Take from me, Lord, whatever displeases Thee, and grant me all that will make me agreeable to Thee. Guide me and ever dispose of me according to Thy good pleasure. Grant me, through the intercession of the blessed Virgin, grace never to offend Thee, but always to do Thy holy will. Give me the perfection which the Society of Jesus requires, that my joy may be full. Fill my soul with that spiritual joy which will enable me to find Thee in everything and everywhere, and merit the martyr's palm. Amen.

II.

Deign, most sweet Jesus, by Thy holy name, to be to me truly Jesus, a Saviour, and to grant me the spirit of the Society of Jesus. Engrave on my heart, I pray Thee, this name beloved, to the end that I may feed on its sweetness and be so inflamed with love of it as to die, most sweet and amiable Jesus, ever invoking this benign, sweet and saving name: Jesus, Jesus! Amen.[1]

Our saintly novice had especially in view two things: an intimate union with Jesus Christ and the perfection peculiar to the Society of Jesus. He advanced so rapidly that his superiors sent him to the college of Lecce to teach, before he had completed his first year of novitiate—a thing which rarely happens in the Society. Need we say he fully justified the confidence placed in him. This trial, instead of causing him to grow remiss, served to spur him forward on the way he had begun, and helped him to acquire that temper of mind which great labors and severe struggles demand, without diminishing in the least that fervor which may be deemed the privilege of beginners. In this work of his sanctification how many noble sacrifices! but, at the same time, what profusion of heavenly graces! Divine Provi-

---

[1] On 26th of January, 1840, Gregory XVI. granted an indulgence of three hundred days to all those reciting these prayers.

dence, ever attentive to the good of this cherished soul lavished on him choice graces. At Lecce, he had for spiritual director the venerable Father Bernardine Realini—a man of rare merit, the process for whose canonization has been for a long time before the Roman Congregations.

Of all the subjects that prepossessed the mind of the young religious, and which he discussed with his spiritual director, the foreign missions held the foremost place.

Should he urge his superiors to send him to Japan, or place himself entirely at the disposal of Divine Providence, ever so benignant in its manifestations towards him? That he should hesitate and doubt may, perhaps, astonish the reader. Every step hitherto taken was but to grasp the martyr's crown by a missionary career: to open the way he had exerted, perhaps, undue ardor and firmness; and now that every prospect brightened and the mission of Japan called aloud for help, he hesitates to offer himself. Is this the young man whose letter to Cardinal Spinola we have read? It is the very same, with the same aspirations, but tempered by greater prudence and a more exact conception of apostolic devotedness. He has learned to submit himself to guidance, and to value only what God wills. He knows that attachment to one's own will vitiates offerings otherwise very acceptable, and that the most brilliant actions may prove to be so many steps in the wrong direction. He awaits the word of command, and places himself in the hands of God as a docile and ready instrument.¹

The venerable Father Realini discerned the spirit of God in these dispositions. He wished the good novice to forestall the decision of the superiors, and promised to write himself to the Reverend Father General, on his behalf, about the matter. Our hero received this answer as if from heaven. It inspired him with such confidence in the accomplishment of his design, that ever after, neither the frequent attacks of sickness to which he was subject, nor the violent tempests he experienced on his voyage to Japan, nor the delays occasioned by the most vexatious circumstances, could shake him.

The young man did not long enjoy the pious conversation of the venerable Father Realini; for he was called to Naples to prosecute his studies. However, the society of the angelic Aloysius Gonzaga, whom he found here, and whose example must have influenced his heart at that decisive moment, more than compensated him for this loss. He was just finishing his novitiate and preparing to consecrate himself to God by perpetual vows; and, to crown his fervor, the feast of the Nativity of our Lord was the day set apart for this solemn act. Who can express the thoughts that then animated this magnanimous soul? With what love did he promise unto Jesus to live and die for his sake?

---

¹ We have here a just idea of "perinde ac cadaver," "ut baculus," other strong expressions which malevolence has frequently exaggerated and worked upon.

IV.—THE STUDENT'S TWOFOLD PROGRESS.

To the two years' novitiate in the Society of Jesus succeed the studies preparatory to the priesthood and other employments, interrupted generally by some years devoted to teaching. Those who embrace this life at an early age have the advantage of being thoroughly formed and fitted for the various duties of the apostolic calling. With this view, as we have seen, Spinola was sent to Naples. There he studied philosophy, and probably applied himself too closely, when he was taken with a distressing cough and raising of blood. Anxious for his health, the superiors omitted nothing. They decided to send him to a more healthy climate to finish his studies. On his way to Milan he spent some time in Rome, in order to follow the lectures of the celebrated mathematician, Father Clavius.

At Milan, care and the influence of a more genial climate enabled him to complete his course of philosophy at the college of Brera, and even to teach a class there for a year. He passed the following years either in the study of theology, or in teaching mathematics, for which he had a special taste.

The saintly student comprehended full well the important place which studies hold in the plan of St. Ignatius. Besides, he knew from the testimony of St. Francis Xavier that none but men profoundly learned and skilled in controversy, were fit for the

Japanese mission.[1] He gave himself with all the ardor inspired by his attachment to the Society of Jesus, to the work which had become his special vocation. Moreover, as he was endowed with remarkable talents, and above all, with a quick and accurate judgment, his success kept pace with his zeal, so much so, that when he had completed his studies he was appointed by his superiors to defend publicly some theses in theology.

Let us now consider the young religious under another aspect, or rather see how he joined science to virtue as required by St. Ignatius, giving due preference to the latter as being superior. For him science was not the end, but a means absolutely necessary to attain the real end of the Society of Jesus, that is the glory of God and the salvation of souls. His companions formed no mistaken judgment on this point, and when after his death they were questioned in regard to his conduct, the unanimous declarations of all exhibited a finished picture of religious perfection; constant fervor, unflinching devotedness, fidelity to the least rules, and untiring patience. His virtue had nothing fitful or too exceptional in it; his zeal was regulated and kept within

---

[1] I think it of the last importance to send here men of superior merit, possessed of virtue, tried virtue, and more than ordinary scientific attainments, which may afterwards gain them admission to the Japanese academies. This mission requires men equally learned and virtuous. . . able dialecticians . . quick to follow up their adversaries when they try to escape, &c.—St. Francis Xavier to St. Ignatius and Father Rodriguez: 1552.

due bounds, but for this very reason he had but greater decision and energy for conceiving and accomplishing great designs. Such perfection is hardly met with in isolated cases; it is the fruit of community life, and is developed in a singular manner by the reciprocal influence of generous hearts. As already remarked, our Lord had conferred a favor of this nature upon Blessed Charles Spinola, in giving him a Father Realini as spiritual director, and a St. Aloysius as living model. What a sight! What an incentive must not the meeting of St. Aloysius and Blessed Charles have afforded the whole scholasticate at Naples! The latter highly felicitated himself on having lived so intimately with his saintly companion, and towards the end of his life, in a letter to the Reverend Father General, he still recalled it with gratitude. In fact, these two great souls influenced one another, and the Blessed Charles lost not a single trait of the model he had before his eyes, and especially did he adopt whatever characterized his saintly companion: a more ardent devotion to the most holy Eucharist, a closer union with Jesus, a longing for labors and sufferings. A few particulars will fully portray his student life.

Devotional exercises are regulated by rule with some severity for the religious of the Society of Jesus during their studies; spiritual advancement is always a capital point with them, but in a body essentially militant, science must also have her rights, which the Superiors are directed to maintain. These regulations the holy student respected, but he gave to prayer a large part of the time left at his own disposal and communicated as frequently as he could obtain permission. Hours of recreation and holidays he spent with a few chosen companions, and like St. Aloysius, he infused into them a ravishing unction. If in conversation the word martyr or cross was mentioned, he beheld himself already in Japan, and then his language, his gestures even became so animated as to influence all hearts.

Love for Jesus cannot exist without a similar feeling for his holy Mother. Blessed Charles venerated Mary with filial love, and on all occasions manifested this disposition so clearly that, notwithstanding his youth, he was for four years appointed to direct the sodality at the Brera College. He even invented a new method of honoring her by a crown, which recalls the benefits of which Divine Maternity was for Mary herself the blessed source: the crown has been preserved, and is another proof of the charming simplicity that is the privilege of pure hearts.

Union with Jesus presupposes mortification. Our Saint derived this axiom from St. Ignatius, and he practised it beyond what human prudence would have permitted. But besides ordinary motives, he was impelled by the ever present thought of a painful apostleship and the necessity of preparing for its severest hardships. He was unsparing, through the confidence he entertained in his future mission. In delicate health, still enfeebled by sickness and hemorrhage, he chastised his body with fasting and scourges. In this, however, some moderation was requisite; but in the matter of humiliation and interior mortification, he was unsparing. Here we touch on the most delicate labor of the spiritual life, a labor to be properly appreciated only by souls seriously engaged in the ways of perfection. To possess the most precious advantages of genius without ever employing them; enjoy the reputation attached to great talents without clinging to it; flee marks of esteem; rejoice at marks of contempt; in a word, voluntarily and before the eyes of the world assume the livery of Jesus buffeted and crucified; such was Blessed Charles's study, such his preparation for the mission of Japan. He wisely dreaded every aliment to vanity: the least self-complacency would have been, in his eyes, a fraud upon his Divine Master's glory. On this point nothing escaped his vigilant and delicate conscience. Examining one day the exercise book of one of his pupils, he found his name mentioned in connection with some mathematical explanation, and at once removed this mark of esteem. We shall hereafter behold him support with angelic patience the grossest insults from men whom it depended on him alone to punish.

In this daily exercise of apostolic virtues the thought of his loved mission never left him; it ruled his whole life; and the better to prepare for it, he awaited only the close of his studies to give himself entirely to zeal for souls. In the course of the scholastic year he seldom had occasions; but in vacation he visited the hamlets to preach the elements of Christian faith and life to the country people. This employment was his delight. He retained, indeed, his preference for Japan as a field of labor, but if obliged to remain in Europe, he proposed, as a worthy son of St. Ignatius, to devote his whole life, if his superiors consented, to catechetical instructions. Yet his zeal was well ordered, he extended it to all who approached him; but to the students and sodalists confided to him, he was all care, all activity. Not satisfied with general exhortations to all, he had appointed hours for each, and already practised the difficult art of directing souls and curing spiritual maladies. With the more valiant he went further; he sometimes took them to the hospitals, to initiate them directly in the most arduous works of charity. His great care produced wonderful effects on the still feeble hearts of youth; young men of the highest nobility, braving all human respect, performed acts of humility and mortification before the very eyes of their fellow students; others renounced earthly advantages, to devote their lives thenceforth only to Jesus in the obscurity of the cloister.

V.—His First Mission as a Priest.

The time had come when, according to the usages of the Society of Jesus, the Blessed Charles was to be promoted to the priesthood. For ten years he had been preparing for it: but on the approach of this awful dignity, he redoubled his fervor. He applied himself first to order wisely all that bears more directly on the sacerdotal life. In order to maintain the respect and attention becoming the recitation of the breviary, he resolved to fulfil that duty kneeling, and it is worthy of remark that even amid the hardships of his Japanese mission, he was always faithful to this early adopted practice. Who can describe the ardor of his devotion, the tenderness of his love at the very thought of the august sacrifice? Let us judge by his care in purifying his conscience. He confessed several times a week, and it is especially noteworthy that in avowing the slightest imperfections he was agitated by such violent grief that his tears flowed abundantly, and his sobs and groans were heard even in adjacent rooms.

This was in 1594. Raised to the priesthood and on the point of completing his studies, Charles had some hope of being sent to the Indies. He renewed his request in writing. As his only answer he was sent to Cremona, in company with some other Fathers.

The work that awaited the evangelical labors in that city comprised what we know now as a Mission; frequent and popular sermons, an earnest exhortation to penance, elementary explanation of the Christian doctrine, public prayers, edifying manifestations, reform of abuses, general confessions and communions, visits to the obstinate, associations for perseverance, etc.

Father Charles entered on these exercises with all the ardor of an apostle, and what is rare in young missionaries, acted with the prudence of a veteran. He at first took as his share the open air preaching and the catechising; and when God had blessed his efforts, he turned his attention to the establishment of two sodalities. He succeeded, though not without difficulty; but this was only the prelude to a far more arduous and important work.

There was then at Cremona, a convent, where the nuns had swerved from the prescriptions of their rule, and where especially the most essential practice of the vow of poverty had fallen into disuse. Each nun enjoyed her revenue and spent it according to her fancy. Disorders of this kind, now, thank God, known to us only by history, are, as all holy reformers admit, the most difficult to eradicate. Nevertheless the young missionary succeeded so completely that the nuns bound themselves by a solemn promise to maintain poverty, in all its rigor, for the time to come. They took this pledge in the presence of a delegate of the Bishop, and to give it still greater stability, they solicited the Bishop himself, as apostolic nuncio to the Emperor of Germany, to affix the seal of his authority. The Bishop was so struck with the result and so grateful to the Society, that he at once took steps to found a college at Cremona, and did not rest till he had secured it a suitable revenue. Thus the spiritual good done to a few nuns by the zealous missionary became a source of sanctification for thousands.

VI.—Preparations for his Departure for Japan.

The Cremona mission was but an essay of the zeal and powers of the Blessed Charles. As it revealed in him the most valuable qualities for distant missions, his superiors asked no further proof, and gave him orders to prepare to set out for Japan. At this intelligence his joy knew no bounds. A laborious apostleship crowned by martyrdom! This was the fulfilment of all his desires, the dream of his youth, the aim of his studies and all his labor. Without losing time in superfluous preparations or farewell visits, he proceeded to Milan, escaped from the tears of his kindred, and arrived at Genoa to take the first vessel sailing to the Indies. His friends and some members of the family pursued him to that port to prevent his departure. The details of this opposition will reveal completely the disposition of the future apostle.

"Why," they said, "this distant mission field? Let him devote himself—exhaust himself even for the glory of God and the salvation of souls; but why go to the ends of the earth to seek what offers here? Does not well-ordered charity require that care should, above all, be taken of those connected to you by so many ties?" "These," replied the Blessed Charles, "have every succor at hand, while the others are completely ignorant of our holy religion; I wish to labor to save these abandoned souls. To this all-sufficient motive, I may add others personal to me." "And may we know them?" "Certainly, but do not be offended. This Japanese mission will have a two-fold influence for my benefit: it will remove the danger resulting from too frequent intercourse with the members of my family, and enable me to escape any honorable position that my superiors might impose upon me."

This language betrayed a will too solidly founded on reason to be easily shaken; they withdrew, but it was only to return ere long to the attack. At last Blessed Charles could feel that he was delivered from all this importunity; the anchor was weighed, the vessel left the port, but it suddenly struck a rock and had to put back for repairs. In the postponement of the voyage by superior force, his kindred and friends would fain see an indication of the will of heaven. They suggested it to him, and the struggle was renewed. But Blessed Charles, more decided than ever, beheld in these embarrassments of every kind, only trials by which God was preparing him for his mission. At the very time that he repressed so constantly the allurements of earthly affections, he had to conquer a very different repugnance that it is also important to note.

When on the point of embarking for Lisbon, the holy missionary had made only strictly necessary preparations, confiding in Providence for the rest; but his kindred, to give a last proof of their attachment, had warmly commended him to the captain of the galley, to secure him a good place and treatment. Now God permitted that the result was just the reverse. By an inexplicable neglect, the highly recommended passenger was placed away down in the hold, among sailors and servants. To crown his mortification, these rude men lost all respect for his priestly character, and, during the whole night that preceded his sailing, he was subjected to the coarsest raillery. It was surely a severe trial, which he might have arrested by a word; he preferred to submit, bearing it not only with patience, and without manifesting any painful emotion, but with sentiments of joy that belong only to souls crucified to the world with Christ. It struck even these insolent men, and it was from them that the details of that night were learned.

Such acts are not isolated; this heroism is acquired only by degrees; it required assiduous meditation and frequent exercise. Blessed Charles had another special motive: he saw in it a preparation for martyrdom. More than ever did he nourish this thought, and devote to it his unavoidable leisure at Genoa. His last dispositions may be seen in the following letter, written from Milan, December 6, 1593, to Father Pompilius Lambertengo, who was probably engaged in collecting documents relating to the martyrs of the Society. We cite the principal passage of this letter:

"These last days, not to lose time, I have collected a Litany of our members who have thus far shed their blood for the faith. In Father Ribadaneira's Spanish life of Father Borgia, I have found the long-sought names of all the forty drowned by the heretics in the sea through hatred of religion.[1] I also found the

---

[1] Blessed Ignatius Azevedo and his thirty-nine companions, put to death by the Huguenots, when on their way to Brazil, in 1570. They were beatified in 1854.

names of more they put to death, for the same cause, in the island of Florida.¹ I send these to you that you may have the complete list, and, mindful of me, commend me to their prayers that I may imitate their virtues. . . . What does Providence design me to do? If we cannot suffer, it will at least delight us to see what others have undergone, and inflame and prepare ourselves by their fire. Oh, when will that time come! O the day, O the hour, O the moment! O Father Pompilius, what consolation even to think in one's heart of the punishment of death endured for Christ! What then will death itself be!" He concludes: "Your Reverence must repay my precious gift by a visit to the most sacred nail of our Lord's cross, and there pray that it may pierce my heart, and retain it fixed at His feet on the cross."

This last trait fully pictures the future apostle. A sincere and simple-hearted devotion is always worthy of respect, but it especially becomes great souls. This alliance of simplicity in sentiment and sublimity in action excites admiration and wins all hearts. This is the character of apostolic sanctity. Blessed Charles, like a John, an Augustine, a Bernard, a Xavier, drank with joy from the Saviour's fountains. It only remained to pour forth from his heart the superabundance of his love.

---

[1] These were Father Peter Martinez, martyred in Florida, near St. Augustine, Father John Baptist Segura, and Louis Quiros, with Gabriel Gomez, Sancho de Zevallos, Scholastics and Brothers Mendez, Desolis, Redondo and Linares, put to death in 1570, near Chesapeake Bay.

PART II.

VOYAGES OF BLESSED CHARLES SPINOLA.

I.—His Apostleship at Sea.

God seems to have designed to give us in the person of Blessed Charles an example of all the obstacles and vexations that can attend the apostolic career. He called him to Japan, yet ordained that he should reach it only after two years of danger and trial. Portugal, Brazil, Porto Rico, and England were to witness his zeal and constancy, his virtue was to shine in the most widely distant, and extraordinary situations. And that no part of this important instruction should be lost, especially on evangelical laborers, we are made acquainted with the details of his adventures by the apostle himself. He will not write Memoirs: that his modesty would not permit, but he will do as most missionaries of the Society of Jesus have done from the time of St. Francis Xavier in a spirit of humble submission, he will render to his Superior an account of his apostolic voyage.[1]

---

[1] To this practice we owe the Jesuit "Relations" so important now to American history, as well as the "Edifying and Curious Letters," which have excited the admiration of the very enemies of

"It is my duty," he wrote to Father Aquaviva, then governing the Society of Jesus, "to give an account to your Paternity of all that concerns our long and painful navigation, and I willingly fulfil it. If this narrative excites your just compassion for your sons, deign also to thank God, with them, for so many favors, and to obtain for them grace to suffer still more for Christ."

What were the sufferings of which he speaks so simply to his Superior, and what was his conduct during these trials, in the apostolic, novitiate, to use his own expression? His account will inform us.

We left the holy missionary at Genoa, longing for the moment when he was to start for Japan. At length all is ready; the signal for departure is given. They steer gaily towards Spain, and after encountering a storm, arrive at Barcelona. This was only the first station of this interminable voyage: the second portion was more painful. At this time supremacy on the sea was held by the Portuguese; India was a Portuguese possession, and the surest if not the only means of reaching it was to sail from Lisbon. No time was to be lost, if they wished to arrive at this latter place before the departure of the

---

Christianity, and to which the Annals of the Propagation of the Faith are professedly a continuation. St. Francis Xavier's letters contain most just and exalted views on the apostolic ministry; many others, such as those relating to China, are indispensable to history. The value of the letters of Father de Smet in our own day, is too well known to need more than a reference here

India fleet. The Blessed Charles Spinola was consequently obliged to cross the whole Peninusla on foot and with all expedition. But the desire of seeing his beloved Mission lightened the way, and he entered Lisbon at the moment when all the preparations for departure were completed.

There were eight missionaries of the Society of Jesus destined for the same place. To turn the tedious voyage to advantage, they took two different vessels, three in one and five in the other. Father Spinola was among these latter, as well as Father Jerome de Angelis, who shared his labors and martyrdom, and Father James de Vicariis, a venerable man, who died before reaching his Mission. On the 10th of April, 1596, the two ships, accompanied by four others without counting the smaller vessels, sailed out of port, and the passengers for the last time, as they thought, saluted the shores of Europe. There are few, even among the Saints, who, in similar circumstances, do not experience some oppression at heart.

The Blessed Father wrote as follows to the General of the Society:

"In proportion as we receded from land our hearts overflowed with joy. We seemed at that moment to die entirely to the world; we were severing ourselves, even bodily, from our relatives, our friends, and our acquaintances."

The voyage commenced most favorably. In a few days the fleet was off the coast of Guinea, and, on the

26th of May it crossed the line. During a month and a half there were, however, intervals of dead calm and violent winds. They even encountered serious dangers, but all this only contributed to the pious designs of the missionaries. The crew was so free from anxiety that some regular religious exercises were established, and yet there was care sufficient to induce them to attend them eagerly. Twice a day, the soldiers and sailors assembled to hear the Christian doctrine explained. The chanting of the psalms and hymns by hundreds of voices in the immense solitude of the ocean, rose up to heaven with a grand and solemn effect; numerous confessions were heard previous to the festivals of the Ascension and Pentecost; the authority of the Fathers was universally respected. Father Spinola, in particular, had acquired such an ascendency over these rude beings, that he succeeded one day in allaying a violent outburst of passion.

"A quarrel had arisen," writes he, "for I know not what reason, between the soldiers and sailors; they were assembled in two parties, armed with oars and swords, and ready to imbrue their hands in each other's blood. I threw myself into their midst and succeeded in making them lay down their arms, to the great satisfaction of everybody."

The moment was at hand when the Fathers were to regard themselves as fortunate in possessing the confidence of the crew and passengers. For some time past, they had been shaping their course for

Brazil, hoping to meet with winds which would carry their vessel to the Cape of Good Hope, and they daily traversed as much as two degrees in this direction. On the 16th of June, the tropic of Capricorn was crossed, and the vessel was turned in the direction of the Cape.

They were already reckoning the time that must elapse before arriving there : with the favorable wind then blowing, said they, no more than about eight days would be required ; and they were preparing to encounter the storms that prevail in these regions, when a most serious accident blasted all their hopes. One evening when about midway between Brazil and the Cape, a violent wind suddenly broke the rudder, thereby causing indescribable confusion. At first, they thought themselves irretrievably lost, and many, under this impression, hastened to reconcile themselves with God. It was only later that some of the others followed their example, being subdued, as it were, by the accumulation of evils. For, if the vessel did not sink, it remained unable to proceed, thereby leaving the crew a prey to that most unhealthy climate. A sort of pestilence soon broke out on board ; there were numerous cases of hemorrhage ; and still, as if God were desirous of manifesting his merciful views, there were only about ten deaths in all. The missionaries, together with the succors of their holy ministry, lavished every species of consolation on all these sufferers, on those whom this state of affairs plunged into the deepest melancholy, and on those in particular who lamented the ruin of their commercial hopes.

Meanwhile, the leaders of the expedition deliberated on the plan to be adopted in this juncture of affairs. The account given by Father Spinola presents a sufficiently striking picture of what frequently takes place in more important assemblages. They were divided on plans which were equally impracticable. "Let us return to Lisbon," said the captain. "What!" answered another, "without a rudder, venture to undertake so long a voyage? Impossible!" "It is as easy to continue our voyage to India as to return to Lisbon." In fact, in either plan, a new rudder was required, and they resolved on making one forthwith; but neither the necessary workmen nor iron could be found. They supplied the deficiency as best they could, by means of two large pieces of wood placed astern one on each side; and thus, with great care, they were able to steer in favorable weather. And yet, to accomplish even this, the assistance of the soldiers had to be called in, and they were obliged to shape their course once more for Brazil.

The unavoidable delay occasioned by this, the general discouragement, the additional labor imposed upon the men untouched by sickness, all these things contributed to the rapid spread of the disease. Provisions, too, began to run out; they lacked medicines as well as men. The vessel became a pest-house; and at one time there were only ten men fit for duty on board. The Fathers, too, had been attacked.

Father Spinola escaped with a few days' illness, which, to him, were days of rest; after which, with new devotedness, he resumed his attendance on the sick. With no other assistance than that of Father de Angelis, he went among the sick, affording them such assistance as was indispensable.

In this extremity, what was to become of the ship, left almost without any guidance to unexperienced hands? But Father Spinola ceased not to pray. "We were celebrating the anniversary of that day on which, many years before, Father Rudolph (Aquaviva) had suffered death for Jesus Christ, and on which forty other missionaries of the Society had met with the same fate, for whom I had always felt a great devotion. Then recollecting that it was into this very same part of the ocean that they had been cast by heretics, in hatred of the faith, they were ever before my mind." The following night, the vessel was amidst the breakers and on the point of wreck, when an apparently fortuitous circumstance attracted the attention of the crew to their imminent danger: a suspicious-looking craft had come in sight, and, whilst watching it, they became aware of a more serious peril. A slight impulse was that instant given to the ship, and, instead of being wrecked, it entered All Saints' Bay on the 15th of July. Three months consequently had elapsed since their departure from Lisbon.

As soon as it was known in the city that a ship destined for the Indies had arrived in port, the Fathers of the college hastened to welcome the missionaries with that charity which has ever united the members of the Society of Jesus. Under their care, the sick began to recover their strength and vigor; even Father de Vicariis, who had suffered extremely during the voyage, seemed to have improved considerably; but this worthy priest was ripe for heaven. He died a few days after, greatly regretted by all, especially by Father Spinola, who lost in him his most valuable assistant. "How many hours we passed together conversing on heavenly things! What a happy influence his voice and example exerted over my soul! His presence alone did me good." It was in these terms, somewhat later, his sentiments of esteem and affection for this Father overflowed in his letter to the Father General; for, at the time, he was occupied with the care of the sick and innumerable details incident upon a landing under such circumstances. His charity extended to everything; he hesitated not to descend into the hold of the ship, where for the second time he inhaled the germs of disease. He was troubled with nausea, dizziness and fainting fits; these symptoms were certainly discouraging, but still, by the special protection of God, at the end of a week, he was able to resume his occupations. After five months spent in Brazil, the missionaries once more started for the Indies on the 12th of December. Their ship was accompanied out of port by several other vessels, for the most part Belgian, which were soon out of sight in another direction. This second voyage was not more fortunate than the preceding one. Up to the month of March, their progress was slow indeed, but still unattended by any serious accident. But at this time the weather became threatening. A dead calm prevailed, meteors seemed to fall, and all the phenomena announced a fearful storm. After three days, the tempest burst in all its fury, covering the vessel with enormous waves. Great was the consternation ; for it was discovered that the vessel had sprung a leak, and that there were already nearly seven feet of water in the hold. The sails were at once furled, and all set to work at the pumps ; search was made for the leak. That the water entered astern was all that could be clearly made out. There was no direct and efficacious remedy! The pumps had to be kept working day and night. Soldiers and sailors succeeded each other without interruption; but this could not last. Moreover, the vessel was unable to resist the waves ; to lighten it, eighty hogsheads of sugar were thrown overboard, and it was allowed to follow the direction of the wind. In this manner they ran a hundred leagues in constant danger of going down : for three days, they remained, as it were, suspended by a thread over the abyss; "and this time again," writes Father Spinola, "we were saved by the intercession of our holy Martyrs, whom I ceased not to invoke." A profound impression was produced upon all minds by having death continually before their eyes, and by experiencing the sensible protection of Heaven. Both soldiers and sailors—those rude but still simple and upright men — recognized the intervention of Providence :

they humbled themselves beneath the mighty hand of God and answered his appeal by a sincere return to Him. As a proof of this may be adduced the fact that those who were unable to make their confession while the storm lasted, hastened to do so, when no longer urged by any transitory fear. As regarded the missionaries, they were only too happy to gather these precious fruits of salvation. They remained calm and resigned, despite the most terrible privations, and making themselves all to all, blessed the designs of God.

At last the tempest ceased, and, on the 24th of March, the vessel, to the great astonishment of the sailors, came in sight of Porto Rico. As they were not acquainted with the coast of that island, they called in a pilot who took them into port on the feast of the Annunciation of the Blessed Virgin.

II.—Mission of Porto Rico.

Porto Rico, one of the first conquests of the Spaniards in the new world, is one of the Great Antilles. It covers an extent of fifty-four leagues by twenty-four; its population, however, has never reached 200,000 inhabitants. At the time it was visited by our missionaries, the population was divided in the proportion of about four negroes to one white man. The island contains gold, but the extraction of this mineral was regarded as too difficult and expensive. The Spaniards generally preferred to employ their negro slaves on sugar plantations, whose products, owing to the vast extent of the domains of the house of Austria, found a good market in Belgium and Germany. The northern extremity of the island is particularly suited for commercial and military establishments. The sea penetrating into the land, describes a circuit in such a manner as to form a large bay which encloses within its bosom a small island, on which is built the city of San Juan de Porto Rico. This is the capital of the colony, the residence of the principal civil, military and ecclesiastical authorities.

The missionaries were received by the bishop and governor with the consideration due to their character and situation. They only availed themselves of this regard to make themselves useful. They lodged at the hospital, and lived on the food furnished them by the charity of the faithful, persuaded that here especially hearts were to be brought to God by the most austere disinterestedness. Enough has been said about slave countries. Some historians, but particularly some novelists, have greatly exaggerated matters, presenting exceptions as the general rule. The matter is sufficiently gloomy; simple truth suffices, and none have presented this more fairly than the Catholic missionaries, none especially have been at so much trouble, have made more strenuous efforts to apply the true remedy to the evil. Those who have read the life of the Blessed Peter Claver, the Apostle of the Negroes, have formed an exact idea of the lot of these wretched beings, and Porto Rico was, upon a small scale, another Carthagena. Faith was intact, or rather heresy had been carefully excluded, but morals were in a deplorable state. Father Spinola appreciated the position with remarkable precision, and he has described it by two expressions that picture alike whites and negroes. "The indifference of the whites and the ignorance of the blacks have multiplied crimes. It was a special design of Divine Providence that sent us here to wrest a multitude of souls from hell!"

It was just the season of Easter. The missionaries, furnished with the most ample facilities by the bishop, took their places in the confessionals and found night and day a field for their zeal. The crowd was great, but the conversions were not sufficiently prepared. "Ah!" cried the Blessed Charles, "if we but had a pulpit at our disposal!" but it was occupied by the ordinary Lenten preacher, whose powerless voice, like the well known sound of the bell, was lost amid the general indifference. After his departure the missionaries began to instruct the people in another tone, in Portuguese and Spanish. Father Spinola adopted the simplest form, and taught catechism not only in the church but on the streets, wherever he could collect a few hearers. He succeeded in fixing the attention of grown men as if they were children, of men of rank, and especially of the soldiers, to whom the governor was so well disposed as to give every opportunity and the influence of his own example. It was a great happiness for them, for the garrison was soon after decimated by one of those pestilent fevers that so frequently ravage those parts.

The fruits of salvation just reaped in St. John, Porto Rico, inspired the thought of renewing the whole island by a general mission. It could be done without loss of time, nothing being ready for the continuation of their voyage. Moreover, in many parishes, the people had not fulfilled their Easter duties, from want of a valid parish priest or a priest capable of discharging his functions. The mission was accordingly decided upon and the labor divided.

The Father Superior remained near the port to oversee everything and be at the bishop's disposal. Father Alexander Ferrati, with one companion, proceeded to the heart of the sugar plantations and the hovels of the negroes employed in them. These wretched slaves offered no obstacles to the ministers of Christ except the inertia of gross and brutalized ignorance. Once instructed and gained over, they crowded around the confessionals, and took from their hours of sleep the time required by the exercises of the mission. We omit the details of this part of the mission to follow the labors of Blessed Charles.

It fell to his lot to visit the whole island with his faithful companion, Jerome de Angelis, and everywhere to rekindle the Christian spirit. The field was vast and the difficulties of every description. It is an island of a thousand square leagues of surface, without roads worthy of the name, traversed by several ranges of mountains, intersected by innumerable watercourses, which frequently, when swollen by the tropical rains, rolled tumultuously down. Blessed Charles nearly lost his life. He was crossing the same torrent for the twenty-first time, when his horse lost his foothold and was swept down; he himself, spent with fatigue, was carried down a considerable distance, and only escaped by grasping a jutting rock with a last effort. At other times the very roads were changed into streams, and they had to wait for daylight till the waters had subsided, then lie down on the moist earth wet to the skin, and with no shelter but a hastily constructed cabin of palm branches. In the cities they found a sort of bread, and even meat; but in the country they were obliged to live on plantains and a little milk.

The first town visited by our two missionaries was Cramo, in a fertile plain near the southern shore. The inhabitants received them as angels sent from heaven. Their parish priest was sick; yet here, suddenly, two religious men appear, of an unknown order, to prepare them for a worthy celebration of the feast of Whitsunday. Whites and blacks flocked in from four or five leagues around, and, for ten days, put up with every privation, to have the happiness of hearing the word of God and putting their conscience in order. The fruit corresponded to this eagerness. All learned the essential points of Christian doctrine, especially what relates to contrition and confession. They practised them so well that most of them made general confessions with tears, and concluded by restitutions and reconciliations, evincing still more clearly the sincerity of their repentance. Some reflections on the last end of man had sufficed to make them accept any sacrifice, even that of their superstitious practices. This abuse is always difficult to eradicate, when united, as in this case, to extreme ignorance. On this occasion the zealous missionary displayed a great knowledge of the human heart. Not satisfied with destroying the objects employed superstitiously, he replaced them by objects and practices of good and solid devotion, by blessed and indulgenced medals, sprinkling of holy water, etc. He went farther; always guided by the good will and religious tendencies of his hearers, he impressed on them respect for all that concerns divine worship, inspired them with zeal for the house of God, and induced them to roof over their church, to provide it with altar plate and secure some permanent revenue. He obtained all he asked, and when about to depart could not refrain from mingling his tears with the tears of these good people.

His mission was an epoch in the life of the apostolic man. For the first time he bore alone the responsibility of the work, as he had the main share of the toil, his companion not being a priest. It was, therefore, in some respects, his first mission—a mission crowned with the greatest success, and in which he had the joy, as he himself in all simplicity states, of marking the first fruits of his apostleship by conferring holy baptism on a child.

The method here followed he observed in the other localities visited by him, and always with equal success. A true son of St. Ignatius, and early formed in his school, our young missionary had made a profound study of the book of Spiritual Exercises, making them the basis of his missions or retreats. Faithful to the spirit of his holy Master, his instructions were a perfect chain, but he did not adapt them to a given text, or make them a uniform and unvarying theme: he had learned from the very book of St. Ignatius to modify his course and instructions according to the requirements of his hearers. Neither a slave to routine, nor an innovator, and vigorously wielding the spiritual arms—such was, in his eyes, a true missionary, and such he showed himself from the outset. His hearers were ignorant, and to some extent devoid of intelligence; they differed in tastes and manners as much as they did in race and condition. Hence he divided them into groups, gave much space to elementary instruction and insisted on a small number of fundamental truths. On one single occasion he swerved partially from this plan, and resorted to those vivid demonstrations that set a whole community in motion. He had this time met a more cultivated and reserved population. In this he did not act on any preconcerted plan or from system; he allowed himself to be influenced by the event, and yielded to the inspiration of heaven. He thus averted the danger of those great movements which injure when they fail, and he rendered the impression, to some extent, irresistible. We shall now behold him in his labors, displaying in them talents not expected from his exact and positive mind.

After visiting Bucanas, the missionaries reached a district called, by the Spaniards, New Salamanca. Here Blessed Charles proceeded to the exercises of the mission with his ordinary prudence. As usual he confided the explanation of the Christian Doctrine to his young companion, who excelled in that branch. Words full of unction, and untiring patience, drew to the catechist's lessons persons of every age and rank. The children and the negroes took such pleasure in them, that they afterwards gathered together, to talk them over, and imbibe more deeply what they had heard. Nor did the other exercises give less satisfaction. Sermons, confessions, communion, all went regularly with fervor but with calmness. As the mission proceeded, an extraordinary animation arose. People flocked in from the neighboring towns, as they said, to hear the preacher whom God had sent to convert them. In fact, he felt himself impelled by an invincible power: he remarked, with astonishment, that the best thoughts and most effective arguments came to him suddenly and without study. His hearers said that his exhortations enkindled in their hearts an ardor for virtue such as they had never before experienced, and their conduct corresponded to their words. Women returned to the ways of modesty and simplicity: men to piety and practices of penance. Some scourged themselves to blood, and the streets resounded nightly with the sound of these voluntary chastisements. At the sight of such fervor the holy missionary resolved to give full vent to his own feelings and those of the people.

He announced a solemn torchlight procession on the night of St. Barnabas' day, in order to implore of God pardon for their sins and perseverance in their good resolutions. This was an unique spectacle. To read the details given by the holy missionary, one would deem it descriptive of a scene in Italy itself.

The procession was composed of all the able portion of the people. Almost all the men came barefooted, and several scourged themselves to blood; some women, veiled to avoid recognition, followed the whole way on their knees, while others filled the air with their cries and lamentations. With these moving manifestations were intermingled, from time to time, the voices of children chanting in a mournful tone, "Mercy, Lord Jesus, mercy!" The emotion grew more intense, and it overpowered all, the missionaries as well as the people. On re-entering the church, Father Charles could not refrain from addressing a prayer to Jesus crucified, but his voice was drowned in tears. The people replied by sobs, by protestations of fidelity, by repeated scourgings, by scenes of repentance that were prolonged till dawn of day.

The fruit of the mission was not unworthy of the extraordinary demonstrations that had accompanied it; the holy missionary giving the best proof. Towards the close of the mission, which lasted a whole month, those who returned to the tribunal of penance had to accuse themselves of no fault resembling their former transgressions. To persevere thus, till death, seemed now easy, and they promised to do so, provided some one came once a year to remind them of the truths of salvation. How often are not missionaries obliged to hear the touching invitation to return, and often and frequently are able to answer only by a kind prayer and a warm recommendation. The harvest is abundant, but the laborers are few—holy laborers especially. Send, O Lord Jesus, into thy vineyard, men according to thy divine Heart.

After this holy excursion, our two missionaries returned to Porto Rico, laden with merits and followed by the blessings of the inhabitants whom they had evangelized. Then the consequences of excessive toil began to show themselves. He who had borne the chief burthen was seized with a fever, but after some days seemed sufficiently restored to embark with his companions.

III.—A Prisoner in England.

The ship in which our missionaries had reached Porto Rico, was repaired, but still far from seaworthy. After the twice-repeated experience of its defects, they resolved to select another means of conveyance. Several vessels were ready to set sail in the same direction: this time, too, the missionaries divided, and Blessed Charles, with his mission companion, was appointed to go in a new light vessel, but small and poorly armed, carrying only two iron cannon, and not a man able to work them. According to his custom he begged what he required for his subsistence, and although still suffering he embarked.

Eight vessels cleared together from the harbor of Porto Rico, August 21, 1597, but two days after so furious a tempest arose, that it separated the vessels and dispersed the whole fleet. That carrying our two missionaries, by chance, fell in with a Belgian merchantman, full of Spaniards and Portuguese, at the time subjects of the same prince. Communication was opened, and the merchantman, which was in very poor condition, obtained a promise to sail together for mutual protection and in case of accident. This concert caused the loss of the Portuguese ship.

In the first place, they had to regulate its course by that of the Flemish ship, which greatly retarded it, and sometimes made it lose as much as ten leagues a day. The navigation was prolonged by these delays beyond what had been anticipated, and they began to run out of provisions. Fortunately they could at least obtain water, and fish, in great abundance, took the place of meat.

On the 17th of October, the two vessels, in company, passed the Azores, when a sail was seen near St. Mary's, the island nearest Portugal. The first rays of light showed it to be English, and about three leagues off. Every English vessel was an enemy to the subjects of Philip II., and on both sides every capture was declared a lawful prize. It was, therefore, now to be seen whether they were to hope or fear. The captains held a council.

The small Portuguese vessel might have escaped the danger by flight, especially as in that case the English ship would certainly have pounced on the merchantman, and given up the chase of the other vessel. But to abandon a friendly ship to the pirate seemed dishonorable, while, by remaining together, they might either awe the enemy, or fight with him at an advantage. The latter considerations prevailed, and it was resolved to wait for the enemy.

The English ship bore down. It was but a small vessel and lightly armed; but it was guided with the skill and boldness of a pirate, who, in spite of appearances, saw at a glance the inferiority of his opponents. As soon as the merchantman was within range, the pirate opened fire. The former, forced to protect his hull, answered feebly, and his few and ill-served guns produced very little effect. After two hours' action, its sails were so damaged, that further resistance was impossible. Then the Portuguese captain thought of flight, but it was too late. The Englishman gave chase and soon was in possession. When he had accomplished this, he turned his attention to the merchantman; but the latter had disappeared, and was not seen again. God had apparently provided our apostle with a new opportunity to suffer and to glorify him before sending him to Japan.

Immediately on boarding the ship, the conquerors seized the property of the passengers. A soldier, having forced his way into Father Spinola's cabin, demanded his money sword in hand, and robbed him of four hundred pieces of gold given by the Sovereign Pontiff for the Japanese Missioners. This was only the prelude of a general pillage. Trunks were broken open and searched; books, manuscripts, reliquaries and beads were carried off and divided; nothing was left to the Fathers but the clothes they wore. Such outrages naturally gave rise to fears of some desperate act of retribution on the part of the passengers who had been robbed. For this reason the English captain transferred them to his own ship on the following morning. The Fathers attired in the habit of their order were received with courtesy. Two interpreters in presence of the captain questioned them in Latin as to their country and profession. Here was a welcome chance for one who aspired after martyrdom. Father Spinola knew that the very name of "Jesuits" was an object of hatred to the Protestants: Might not the show of courtesy, with which they were received, be a mask for refined cruelty? Was it not a bitter mockery? Did not the death of Blessed Ignatius d'Azevedo and his thirty-nine companions, warn them of the fate in store for themselves? Thoughts like those, we are informed by his letter, crossed the mind of this hero of Christian faith. They filled his soul with joy, and he declared in terms bold and straightforward, that they were "Italians and members of the Society of Jesus." After this answer all expected to be attacked and ill-used in every way. How great, therefore, was their surprise, when they found themselves treated with the greatest kindness and regard. The captain, with an air of great deference, ordered a cabin next to his own to be given to our Saint, and several times even served him with his own hands. Moreover, he allowed him to go from vessel to vessel to relieve the sick; and he ordered everything that had been taken from him to be restored. In fact, his manuscripts, his crucifix, and some relics, things of no great material value, were restored to him; but the pirates kept what was valuable. Their conduct, however, with all its apparent contradictions, was marked by a spirit of rapacity. One of the interpreters had contracted a friendship with the Fathers. He had received from them some objects, which he wished to show to his mother, who was, he said, a fervent Catholic, and he had offered to keep for them all that had been restored to them, swearing solemnly to restore all to them on his return to England. This was a new way of robbing them. No doubt it was God's wish thus to detach them from all things, even from objects of devotion. So thought the Blessed Charles, who found in every occurrence new reasons for blessing the Divine goodness.

The English captain, satisfied with his success, resolved to make sure of his prize, valued at upwards of twenty-six thousand dollars, and set sail for England. Much as he dreaded storms, it was evident there was something else which he feared still more. He felt uneasy while passing the coast of the continent; and some circumstances which delayed his entry into the Channel increased his alarm. He feared meeting an English vessel as much as he dreaded falling in with a Spanish man-of-war. The nearer he approached his goal, the more apparent became the illegal character of his doings. Finally, on the 5th of November he cast anchor at Yarmouth. His arrival was a subject of great rejoicings to the people of the town. Still greater was the joy when the captain proceeded to his native place, where he seemed inclined to make a longer stay.

Henceforth the situation of the missionaries became better defined. The captain assigned them separate quarters, and paid for the support of each two shillings a day. They could take their meals and go through their devotions in their rooms without being watched; in short, they were better treated than any other prisoners. Gradually they extended the sphere of their activity. From all sides visitors came to see the captain, some to pay their respects, others to transact business with him. Some of these also visited the Fathers. Those who spoke Latin, Spanish, or Italian conversed with them, and, charmed by their courteous address, they soon passed to more serious subjects, and opened friendly discussions on the religious questions which absorbed every one's attention during the sixteenth century. In England, where on the most idle pretexts, the sovereign had inaugurated the rebellion against the authority of the Church, it had been found necessary to deceive the people regarding Catholic doctrines. The most absurd fictions, the basest slanders had become deeply-rooted prejudices. Even at the present day, many English people sincerely believe that the Papists, to use their own expression, are idolaters, who adore the Saints and their images, and fanatics who reduce the conversion of sinners to a mere external form, nay, to a question of money; the Fathers were pleased to undeceive their visitors on these points. Their happiness was still greater when, even in this desolate country, they met with some Catholic families. They found them worthy of the trials which they had undergone, unshaken in their attachment to the Church, and loved and esteemed even by their Protestant neighbors.

Such a life, however, had few charms for the generous heart of the Blessed Spinola. He therefore asked the captain to allow him to go to London or to some other port, whence he might sail for Lisbon. The captain had no reason to deny his request, but he distrusted the Father's intentions. Instead of leaving the country, these strangers might lodge complaint at London for the purpose of obtaining the restitution of their property, or, what seemed even more dangerous, they might seek to re-establish the Catholic religion in England. If this should prove to be the case, their temerity would expose the man who had brought them to England to the full rigor of the laws then in force against Catholics. In fact, the edicts of Queen Elizabeth far surpassed in intolerant cruelty anything that has been charged against the Spanish Inquisition. Frightened by the mere possibility of running such risks, the captain strictly forbade the Fathers to leave the city. In vain his friends and relations spoke in their favor; their entreaties only increased his suspicions. He knew that there were many Catholics who escaped by the payment of money the legal obligation of attending Protestant churches, and who secretly favored the practices of Catholicity. Men of this stamp need only come in contact with the zealous missionary, who took no pains to hide his burning desire to celebrate at least once the sacrifice of mass on English soil, and the captain's head would pay for the favor asked of him. Judged by his own standard he was right; but the missionaries, wrongfully deprived of their freedom, could no longer bear their forced inactivity.

At one time they thought of making their escape, and of devoting themselves to promote in England the cause of Catholicity, so nobly upheld by the Campians and the Southwells. Two considerations induced them to abandon the project. In the first place, they were unacquainted with the English language; secondly, they could hardly hope for the palm of martyrdom in England. As strangers, brought to England against their will, the most they could expect was expulsion from the country. For these reasons they concluded to abide by their first resolution, and to return as soon as possible to Lisbon. When they spoke directly of this, the captain, instead of opposing their views, did his best to aid them. As they were obliged to disguise themselves, to escape the hatred of the fanatics and the searches of informers, he procured for them lay dress; but, always a prey to distrust, he at the same time ransacked their baggage, to prevent their carrying with them letters or other objects that might compromise him. Having found nothing suspicious, he allowed them to depart.

On the 5th of December the missionaries embarked, but fearful storms awaited them. So it had been for two years. Scarcely had the vessel reached the ocean, when, as if by Divine interposition, the winds spent all their fury to prevent them from reaching their goal. They had to bear all the rage of the elements. They suffered, were numbed with cold, and wet through by the waves, which continually swept the deck. "At no time during this expedition," writes Father Spinola, "did we suffer so much as during the two days during which this storm raged; and at no time did we experience heavenly consolation so pure and so sweet. The sailors made unheard of efforts to reach an island hard by; they could not succeed, and, worn out by their exertions, put back to another English port."

On landing at this part of the English coast, which is not clearly described by Father Spinola, they congratulated themselves on being disguised. The Queen having issued still more vigorous edicts against Catholics, and ordered them to be treated with the most unrelenting severity, they would not have escaped a long imprisonment had they been recognized. It was necessary therefore to provide for speedy re-embarkation. They applied, in the first instance, to two Italian captains—the one from Genoa, the other from Ragusa. They were very charitable men, and offered to take the Fathers to Leghorn; "but I refused this offer," says the Blessed Spinola, in his letter to Father General, "fearing that, being under your immediate control, your paternity might oppose our departure for the mission, which was the goal of our ambition." They found another captain, who was willing to take them to St. Jean de Luz, on the confines of Spain and France, whence they could reach Lisbon by land. They were on the point of accepting his proposal, when they fell in with a safer and more expeditious means of making the voyage. They met a German merchant, who, by the permission of the King of Spain and the Queen of England, conveyed the prisoners exchanged between the two nations. This man proved very obliging, and, having agreed upon the terms, he prepared to depart; before weighing anchor, however, the Fathers were doomed to new trials.

They had already undergone many spiritual privations, rendered necessary by prudence. They had been unable to say mass on Christmas day; but, writes the Blessed Spinola, "it would have been wonderful that two priests should leave England without having suffered imprisonment for Jesus Christ." They lodged at the house of a woman, who treated them well, hoping that, on their arrival at Lisbon, they would help her to effect an exchange of her husband for a Spanish ensign, whom she held as a hostage. This ensign, equally desirous to obtain his freedom, had written letters to his friends and entrusted them to the Fathers. This circumstance, which became known, caused them to be suspected of carrying other letters; and forthwith their rooms were entered by night and their baggage searched. Luckily nothing else was found; but the examining parties, having heard the Blessed Jerome de Angelis say something in Italian, took him for a Spaniard, seized him and put him in prison. Nevertheless, only one night remained. The rest were subjected to some measures of precaution and a formal examination; after which the missionaries, to their great joy, went on board at the beginning of January, 1598, and, though the vessel was old and ill-equipped, they reached Lisbon in eight days.

They proceeded at once to the Professed House, where their arrival was greeted with no less surprise than joy. They had resided there two years previously, but they were not recognized at once. Their disordered hair, their uncouth beards, their rude attire—in fact, their whole appearance, proclaimed them sailors rather than religious. But as soon as it became known who they were, they were welcomed the more heartily, as their fate had so long been a mystery. They were pressed to relate their adventures, and to edify their brethren by the story of their sufferings. In this recital our young apostle displayed all the fervor of his devotion, all his love of the cross of Christ. He spoke as another St. Paul, enumerating the perils through which he had passed in his apostleship—perils on sea and on land, perils of robbers and of false brethren, in weariness and painfulness, in hunger and thirst, in cold and nakedness—nay, in danger even of death.—II. Cor. xi. 25. His tattered garments added to the effect of his words, for he wore them with apostolic pride as the livery of Jesus Christ, and in his own words he had never seen himself so well dressed.

After satisfying the pious curiosity of his brethren, the holy religious retired into the obscurity of community life, and combined with great industry a striking faithfulness to all his obligations as a religious.

IV.—Arrival of Blessed Charles in Japan.

On reaching Lisbon, in January, Blessed Charles had hoped to sail for Japan in the month of April then following,[1] and even before resting from his fatigue, he explained his desire to his superiors. They did not, however, feel able to grant it without consulting the Reverend Father General. Communication was then rare and slow, so that the reply could not reach Lisbon from Rome before the day fixed for the sailing of the fleet. This delay affected the fervent missionary, inasmuch as he conceived great anxiety as to the whole design. Would not this long forced stay in Europe entail difficulties not easily overcome, and encourage his family to renewed in-

---

[1] An autograph letter of B. Charles to his friend F. Lambertengo, at Milan, dated Lisbon, March 21, 1598, and preserved in the library at Amiens, breathes this desire.

stances to retain him? This danger must be met. And the holy missionary acted promptly. After writing to Reverend Father Claude Aquaviva, General of the Society, a long letter from which we have drawn the substance of the three last chapters, he closes it by these expressions, which portray the situation of his soul and are explained by the object he so persistently sought:

"Here we are ready and disposed, more desirous than ever, to continue our voyage, and ready to recommence a thousand times the route we have just taken. We expect sufferings far different from those we have hitherto endured. For myself, I was already accustomed to them, and what seemed difficult to those who had never experienced them seemed very easy to me. Such trust have I in God, that were all human means to fail me, I believe he would give me wings to fly whither I feel He calls so visibly, and for so many years. I know full well how unworthy I am to labor in that noble mission, and I blush when I think of myself amid so many illustrious workmen; yet I hope, cold and hard as I am, that in contact with their fire I shall be inflamed. If God permits me to do anything, He alone shall have the glory, for He alone could have effected it."

While letters thus went from Lisbon to Rome worthy of an apostle, others no less pressing came from Genoa to retain the holy missionary in Europe. The illustrious Spinola family earnestly solicited this favor as a proper act of deference: they cited his ineffectual attempts, which had only served to bring him back to his starting point. Was not this a token of God's will, and was it not sufficient for the good religious to have evinced his devoted zeal? Specious as these motives were, they could not counterbalance the dispositions of the earnest missionary, especially on a mind so superior as that of Father Claude Aquaviva. He withstood the family of the apostle and renewed his permission to him and his companion to proceed to Japan. He added another favor, or rather act of justice, by admitting the holy religious to his solemn profession. As is well known, profession, in the Society of Jesus, includes a fourth vow, obliging the professed to go and preach the gospel among infidels and heretics at the first command, and if need be, without any means provided for his support. In this our missionary beheld only that engagement to apostolic self-denial, and he consecrated himself forever to the work which God pointed out to him, with all the joy of his heart. To crown his consolation, his companion, the Blessed Jerome de Angelis, was promoted to Holy Orders.

Both remained at St. Anthony's College awaiting the departure of the fleet, which was not to sail till the next year. Their presence at Lisbon was a disposition of divine Providence, who wished to afford them an opportunity of once more exercising their zeal and charity. The plague suddenly broke out. The Fathers of the Society, as of all time, devoted themselves to the service of those attacked. While some traversed the city at all hours of the day to give assistance wherever it was invoked, and others remained constantly in the church to administer the holy sacraments, our devoted missionary gave his services as lavishly as usual, and gave almost the whole of this year to works of mercy.

At last he beheld the long desired day of departure approach, and he followed the preparations with anxious interest. These preparations were more than usually extensive, as a fleet recently cleared for the Indies had returned to port in shame, not daring to cope with the Dutch. This time seven men-of-war were fitted out to defend the honor of the Portuguese flag against any enemy. It now remained only to provide the passengers and crews with spiritual aid. This was not easy. Men, just from a plague-stricken city, might carry contagion to the fleet, and make each ship a hotbed of incurable infection. At this idea the terrified priests refused to embark. The magistrates then applied to the superiors of the Society, begging them to furnish the necessary chaplains. Twenty were assigned and distributed among the various vessels. Blessed Charles Spinola had with him his old companion, now a priest, and was appointed superior of those who shared his labors on the same ship. They set sail towards the end of March, 1597.

I shall not detail the events of the voyage, during which the holy man discharged all the duties of an apostle with a redoubled zeal drawn from the responsibility of his post. This time he had the consolation of seeing the most consoling practices of religion established on board. The sick, in particular, testified a holy zeal to receive the sacraments; and of these, in consequence of the contagion, there were many. The zealous missionary himself, after bearing up against all this exertion for a long time, was seized with a stubborn fever, which, for two months, so undermined his strength that consumption was feared. He had reached Goa, but seemed incapable of continuing his voyage; but he saw before his eyes the vessel that was at last to carry him to Japan: he invokes Jesus; he was full of confidence which calls forth miracles; he embarks in spite of the fever that consumed him; he bears a long voyage of sixty-five days, during which they ran out of water, and, on reaching Malacca in July, 1600, he found himself, by a signal benefit of God, cured.

At Malacca he received, through the Fathers residing in that city, the first tidings of his beloved mission. That very year several new establishments had been formed in Japan, and the most abundant harvest was anticipated from that vineyard; the workmen, far from sufficient for the harvest, like those in the gospel, implored their comrades to hasten to their assistance. In answer to this appeal the holy missionary urged his departure, disembarked a week after, and, in four months, entered the port of Macao.

Macao belongs to China, but, by its chief inhabitants, by its establishments and civilization, was a Portuguese city. It thenceforth enjoyed several privileges, and greatly facilitated all intercourse between Europe and China. The College of the Society of Jesus was the rendezvous of all the missionaries destined to China or Japan. There they learned the language, the customs, and all that could fit them for their special vocation. Blessed Charles had to pass through this probation also. He was, at the same time, entrusted with the care of the material interests of the Province of Japan, and appointed to superintend the erection of a new church in honor of the Assumption of the Blessed Virgin. His thorough acquaintance with mathematics and the arts of design depending on them, had obtained the latter office, and he drew the plan of the edifice. But his zeal was not content with such labors. He so ardently and successfully cared for the spiritual interests of the Portuguese, that the most important part of the ministry of the word was assigned to him.

There was a usage dating back to St. Francis Xavier, apostle of the Indies and Japan. That great saint had a special devotion for the passion of our Lord, and he often made it the subject of his exhortations. Since then, in all the churches of the Society of Jesus, all the Fridays in Lent were devoted to the exercises of this devotion. In the evening business ceased as on a holiday, and the people crowded to the sermon, which was followed by an expiatory procession. The most striking demonstrations attended these pious exercises: it was not only the profusion of lights and religious emblems, but the public expression of compassion and penance, voluntary flagellation to blood. Amid a people susceptible of great emotions, such ceremonies produced an immense effect. Sinners repaired their scandals, to the wonder of pagans. But to produce these effects required a powerful man; besides natural gifts it required a soul breathing only for Jesus crucified. Such had Father Spinola already shown himself, and, on this occasion, he reaped fruits of penance and sanctification of which the "Indian Letters" of this year exalt the marvels.

These great qualities had attracted the attention of the Superiors of the mission. Father Emanuel Diaz and Valentine Carvalho endeavored to retain him in China, where they saw his extraordinary talent for mathematics would be far more useful than in Japan. But the holy man felt his call to Japan too visibly— and, as he said himself, Japan had cost him too dearly, to renounce it the moment he was about to enter there. Moreover his orders were for Japan, not for China, and, on the first opportunity that arrived, he embarked with his faithful companion, and arrived happily at Nagasaki in the month of July, 1602.

He at last treads the soil of Japan. So often arrested by obstacles of every kind, subjected to trials most painful and most diverse, he reached that land, where he beheld dimly the precious reward of his labors—the martyr's crown. Japan! Japan! Never ceasing to repeat it in his noble aspirations, he uttered it at this moment in the joy of his heart, and blessed the amiable Providence that ordered all things wisely. Let us leave him to his transports, and examine, on the spot, the field of his future labors and sufferings.

PART III.

APOSTOLIC LIFE IN JAPAN

I.—State of the Mission.

Japan, from the time it became known to Europeans, has excited the most intense interest. Those islands, in the remote extremity of Asia, concealed a population whom rare qualities of mind and heart at once commended to the curiosity of Portuguese navigators. In 1549, St. Francis Xavier penetrated into the country amid a thousand obstacles, and founded a Christian church, which, in less than a century, produced the most heroic virtues and a countless army of glorious martyrs.

The mission, in the outset, was a very difficult one. The people promptly conceived the truths proposed, but opposed them with endless subtleties; they showed themselves noble and generous, but haughty and arrogant: moreover, their virtues, as well as their vices, were cunningly turned to account by the bonzes or ministers of the established religion. Had this violent and hypocritical caste been able to rely on a central power universally recognized, they might have long hampered the progress of the gospel; but at that period a civil war had changed the relations of the princes with each other. The head of the army, called the Sama, had reduced the Dairi, or religious monarch, to the position of nominal sovereign, most of the princes becoming independent. Thus Japan became divided into a host of small and mutually jealous kingdoms. The princes who embraced Christianity naturally became the protectors of all the other converts. Such were the prince of Omura and the king of Bungo and Arima, who founded several religious establishments in their states. In 1582 they sent an embassy of obedience to the Sovereign Pontiff, in the name of the new church of Japan. This church then counted, after thirty years' existence, more than 200,000 Christians, governed by a bishop selected from among the missionaries.

The political changes that ensued were not at first prejudicial to religion. The emperor, Nobunanga, who had extended his power over a great part of Japan, was not hostile to religion, and his successor, even, began by protecting them. This was the famous Taico-Sama, who rose from the most obscure position to the first dignities of the empire, then usurped the throne from his benefactor's son, and reunited, under his sceptre, all the kingdoms of Japan.

Taico-Sama was not devoid of genius : he saw through the pagan superstitions, and appreciated the Christian religion ; but an immoral man and a despotic sovereign, he could not long love a religion which inspired women with chastity and men with courage never to obey at the expense of their conscience. In 1587 the Christian virgins of Arima, having repulsed the criminal solicitations of the emperor, this was enough to enkindle his anger and involve all the Christians in his resentment. He instantly ordered General Ucondono, the firmest support of his empire, to depart into exile, and the next day notified Father Coeglio, the Superior of the Jesuits, to leave Japan with all the missionaries under pain of death.

The Fathers decided that they ought not so readily to abandon this flourishing Christian flock. They contented themselves with withdrawing from all public notice and acting with extreme circumspection. The emperor, satisfied with this mark of deference, did not urge the rigorous execution of his orders. He even received with contempt the new king of Bungo, the apostate Joscimon, who had put to death several Christians in his dominions. The return, in 1590, of the Japanese deputies from Rome, headed by Father Valignani, ambassador of the Viceroy of God, tended to conciliate the pacific dispositions of the emperor. This happy state of things entirely prevailed on the news at court of the conquest of the Corea, which the bravery of some Christian generals had achieved. Hereupon Christianity made rapid progress, especially among the nobles, who enrolled with enthusiasm under the standard of Jesus Christ.

Up to 1593, the Jesuits alone, then numbering one hundred and thirty, had cultivated the vineyard of our Lord; but in the month of June, the same year, four religious of the order of Minors of St. Francis arrived at Nagasaki. Admitted as ambassadors of the governor of the Philippines, they soon established friars at Meaco, Osaca, and at Nagasaki. These excellent religious, led only by the burning zeal which animated them, commenced the public exercise of the ministry. This conduct gave rise to hostile rumors, which were aggravated by the boasting of a Spanish pilot. This man being made prisoner by the Japanese, endeavored to intimidate them by an exaggerated account of the power of his sovereign, who, added he, was making use of priests and religious in the conquest of foreign countries. At such news, Taico-Sama hesitated no longer. He ordered the missionaries at Meaco and at Osaca, the two principal cities of the empire, to be arrested. His officers did not stop here. In order to spread terror among the people, they made out the lists of the Christians who frequented the churches. Hereupon a general massacre was expected. Among the three hundred thousand faithful who then formed the Church in Japan, there existed a general enthusiasm for martyrdom. The missionaries shared in this heroism, and they at once appeared at the most threatened posts to sustain the courage of the Christians, when Father Gomez, Vice-Provincial of the Society of Jesus, faithful to the traditions of his order, enjoined upon his subjects to retire to their places of retreat and to exercise their apostleship in secret. But this prudence of a responsible leader did not suffice to check the ardor of the multitude. Their subsequent heroism revived the most brilliant days of the primitive church.

The brave Ucondono, from the court of the king of Cango, returned to Meaco, to die with Father Organtini; a cousin of Taico-Sama, the possessor of three kingdoms, imitated this example; a certain nobleman threatened to punish any of his subjects who should be known to deny the Christian religion; another, fearing he might be spared on account of his rank, went with his wife and two children (the youngest of whom was still an infant) and presented himself with them to the nearest governor. Andrew Ongasavera, of a noble family of Bungo, had his name inscribed on the list of the names of all the Christians at Osaca, with those of his wife and of his father aged eighty years. Sacandono, the eldest son of Genifoin, the viceroy of Meaco, surpassed all others; being at a distance of six hundred miles from the capital, he returned to it in all speed at the news of the edicts of Taico-Sama, and in order to attract more certainly the notice of the persecutors, he assumed the garb of a priest. Constantine, his brother, and Michael, their cousin, notwithstanding the threats of Genifoin and the tears of his spouse, proclaimed aloud that they were Christians, and by their conduct manifested their ardent desire of martyrdom.

Christians of the lower orders of society appeared before the officers of justice with intrepidity; even women rivalled men in courage. The queen of Tango, and at another time the wife of Andrew Ongasavera were found working with their maids preparing more costly robes, in order to appear with more than ordinary magnificence on the day of their triumph, for it is thus they styled that of their martyrdom. But what excited the admiration of all was not only the ardor with which children gave in their names to be inscribed on the lists of Christians which were drawn up, but also their apprehension lest they should escape death. Finally, this movement gradually subsided on the news that none should be put to death except the religious arrested at Meaco and at Osaca with a few Christians. Twenty-six were accordingly crucified at Nagasaki on the 5th of February, 1597. Of this number, there were six religious of the order of St. Francis, Blessed Peter Baptist, their Superior, Blessed Martin de Aguirre of the Ascension, and Francis Blanco, Priests, with three brothers, Philip de Las Casas or of Jesus, Blessed Francis de Parilha or of Saint Michael, and Blessed Gonsalvo Garcia; three Japanese Jesuits, Blessed Paul Miki, Blessed John de Gotto, and Blessed James Kisai; the others were domestics, boys who served at the altar, or catechists under the direction of the Franciscan religious and arrested with them in their houses, or fervent Christians who of their own accord had joined the troop of martyrs. These generous confessors were beatified by Urban VIII. in 1627, and canonized in 1862 by Pius IX.

The year following (1598), Taico-Sama died, and the Church had an interval of peace. The first care of the Bishop Don Louis Secheira, and of the Visitor Father Valignani, was to re-establish the affairs of their diocese and communities. Fresh bands of missionaries arrived from China; thirty new establishments were opened by the Society of Jesus; the Seminary of Nagasaki was reorganized and soon numbered eighty students; they reconstructed the residences which had been destroyed, and new ardor for the holy cause manifested itself in every kingdom. The conversions were numerous. One hundred and twenty thousand infidels were converted and received baptism in the years 1599 and 1600, and this onward movement was far from subsiding.

In 1601 other religious of various orders arrived in Japan to aid with the ministry of their zeal. This same year, for the first time, were native secular clergy found administering to the spiritual wants of this generous people.[1] Some Christian kings, especially in the island of Ximo, labored like true apostles in the conversion of their subjects. Ioscimon, deprived of his kingdom of Bungo, humbled himself under the hand of God, and by his admirable penance repaired the scandal of his apostacy. If calm and peace had thus continued, the entire empire of Japan would have been converted, and what happy results would not thence have followed in the eastern world!

The new emperor, Daïfu-Sama, or Cubo-Sama,[2]

---

[1] The Jesuits are then falsely accused of not being favorable to the formation of native clergy in the country which they evangelized. If they have not done everywhere else what they did in Japan, it is because they did not find subjects susceptible of the same culture.

[2] A great confusion generally exists in the Japanese proper names. We designate the great persecutor by the name *Daïfu-Sama;* *Cubo-Sama* is a more generic appellation.

who had usurped the throne of Findeiory, son of Taico-Sama, did not yet manifest any hostile intentions. On the mediation of the Christian princes, he forbade his ill-disposed governors to oppress the faithful in any way; he went so far as to issue public edicts by which he allowed the Jesuits to form new residences. Some persecutions, however, took place here and there; these were warnings of which God made use to preserve this most illustrious Christian community in its exemplary fervor up to the time of the great persecution.

Before the relation of this terrible trial of the Church in Japan, we shall accompany our Blessed Charles Spinola in his apostolic labors.

II.—COMMENCEMENT OF HIS LABORS IN JAPAN.

The Blessed Charles Spinola, with a band of illustrious missionaries, arrived in Japan during the interval of calm which separates the partial persecution of Taico-Sama from the violent one which signalized the reign of Daifu-Sama. He had then an opportunity of proving the ardor of his zeal before he glorified Jesus by the heroism of his courage. During the first ten years he appeared, in the most varied employments, a perfect model of evangelical laborers; for the ten following years, during the persecution, always above every other interest but that of his divine Master, he displayed in turn the prudence of the serpent and the simplicity of the dove.

The holy missionary was first required to learn the

language of the country. For this purpose he was sent to Arima, the capital of the kingdom of the same name, where the Society had a college; and to afford him more occasions of speaking the language which he learned in the exercise of his zeal, he was thrown into communication with the young Japanese. Of these, such as seemed to be of the most promising dispositions were educated in the seminary then depending on the college of Arima, and which had been transferred from Nagasaki. This seminary was founded and still supported by alms gathered for this purpose in Europe, and by the liberality of John, king of Arima. It was one of the bright hopes of the Church in Japan. Nothing in it was neglected to enable its inmates to become one day the defenders and propagators of Religion among their countrymen. The better to succeed in this, the students of highest merit were admitted into the Sodality of the Blessed Virgin, of which the direction was confided to Father Spinola.

This was a fresh testimony of esteem on the part of his superiors, and the fame of his sanctity must have been well established when like undertakings were proposed to him from every quarter. Here, the future of his dear mission, and of the most precious and efficacious element in the salvation of souls, was concerned. Animated with this thought, the fervent missionary devoted himself unreservedly to the duties of his charge with all the consolation of a great heart inflaming his fellow-men with his own love for Jesus. His direction was, moreover, full of wisdom, and especially adapted to the wants of the Church in Japan. In the midst of this choice Christian community, there was need of saints, of men adequate to the trials and emergencies of the most atrocious persecutions; and from this congregation were to come forth leaders capable of sustaining the others in the confession and defence of the Faith. Thus judged the holy director, and on this judgment were framed rules for the admission and training of the members. He examined the candidates attentively; such as were found to have the required qualities were prepared for their reception by a retreat of eight days, during which time they made a general confession. He seemed to omit no means of enticing them to the formation of solid virtue in their hearts. His great delight was to pass some time after meals in company with these his spiritual children, and to recreate them with spiritual things.

Directions as to the manner of practising mental prayer, the different exercises of mortification, the means of advancing in the most necessary virtues, and analogous subjects which he rendered interesting, furnished him occasions of communicating to these young hearts that divine love with which he himself was so inflamed. An extraordinary fervor among all was the fruit of his solicitude. A young member of the sodality, who had passed but six months under his direction, died in the odor of sanctity.

Our Blessed did not lose sight, however, of the special end of these first occupations, and so at the close of the year he had a sufficient knowledge of the Japanese language to enable him to devote himself entirely to the holy ministry. His virtue and prudence marked him out, moreover, for some important post. His superiors did not think the care of a mission, in the midst of so many difficulties, to be above his capacity and merit.

III.—His Pastoral Functions.

In all the infidel countries, every college is naturally at first a centre of apostolic excursions, then of established parochial residences, around which group the newly converted. The isolated condition of the missionary is in many respects a detriment, and especially so to the preservation of the interior apostolic spirit of the missionaries themselves. In order to maintain this happy fervor, and at the same time to insure unity of action amongst them, it is necessary that on certain days they should come to renovate their spirits among their brethren, concert with them their plans of action, make known their success, expose their difficulties, and receive the advice of their superiors. This method was practised at the college of Arima, whither the missionaries of the surrounding country repaired every two months. At a distance of three miles from this centre was a large town of eight thousand souls, named Aria.

To our Blessed Charles the spiritual care of this place was assigned. He had a companion, though not the beloved disciple who had hitherto shared his toils and dangers. Blessed Jerome de Angelis received another appointment, and rejoined his master only to accompany him to martyrdom. If this separation affected them, they did not evince it, and they doubtless adored the designs of God, who is pleased to purify his elect and elevate them by the sacrifice of earthly affections.

The new pastor of Aria, on assuming the care of others, did not neglect the most important point, his own sanctification. He resolved not to leave his flock without reason, but also never to omit attending the meetings at the Arima College, and there devote the time he could spare to a serious review of his own conscience. Thus disposed he began his labors. For the first time the zealous missionary found what he so ardently desired—a field to cultivate in that land of martyrs; a flock to form and sanctify by all the means that the Saviour has bequeathed to us. He had to provide for all the spiritual wants of these Christians. He was, in all the extent of the word, their good and holy pastor. Yet his ministry had not the lustre which generally environs the steps of the first missionaries in a heathen country, it flattered no illusion, and gave no earthly satisfaction; all was obscure and monotonous; but this was the post that Jesus, his divine Head, had assigned to him—the devoted soldier asks no more.

Most of his time was absorbed by the administration of the holy sacraments, of which he endeavored to render the use frequent and easy. In regard to the sick his care was untiring. At any hour of the day or night that his assistance was invoked, he hastened as though he had nothing else to claim his time. Sometimes, returning fasting from one extremity of his vast parish, he would receive a message summoning him in all haste to the opposite extremity; then, without taking time to touch a little nourishment, his principal food was, after the example of his divine Master, to do the will of Him who sent Him. It was in fact the only thing that could have sustained him amid so great labors, and given him that admirable equality of application and fervor, so difficult to maintain when the body is weary and broken.

The great object of pastoral solicitude, in his eyes, was instruction, especially the elementary instruction of his flock. Ever since his Cremona and Porto Rico missions this conviction had been but strengthened in his mind. He instructed on all occasions. Obliged to restrain his zeal in public, because the storm of persecution still muttered in the distance, he made up for this by extraordinary labor—indeed, in private conversations. He multiplied his visits, he adapted his instructions to the wants of each, and thus infused into some souls not only the most sublime truths but the most heroic sentiments.

A good pastor's care is not confined to spiritual wants, it extends to those of the body also. And the times were hard for many Christians. The persecution had reduced many noble families to indigence, precisely those distinguished by the fervor of their religious sentiments, and who in the days of their opulence had been the pillars of the rising church. Ordinary motives of gratitude were here heightened by gratitude and respect due to confessors of Jesus Christ. After sharing with them his scanty means of existence, the charitable pastor exerted himself among their countrymen and the Portuguese to afford them at least absolute necessaries.

The reader may ask how the holy man was able to undergo so many occupations? And yet the interests of the Christians did not so absorb him but that he found some moments of the day to devote to the idolaters. His ardent zeal received a fresh stimulus from an incident related by himself in a letter to his Brethren in Portugal. One day he was crossing a plain, when at some distance he perceived a crowd around an object that he could not discern. Asking a passer by, he learned that the child of an infidel was dying there a few steps from him before the eyes of the crowd. His course is soon adopted. Dipping his handkerchief in the nearest pool of water, he ran up, pushed aside the spectators, approached the child, and as though administering some corporal remedy, pressed out the water on its head pronouncing the sacramental words. The child thus baptized died some hours after. The holy man felt so much joy at saving this soul, that by this conquest alone, to use his own expression, he felt amply repaid for all his past and future labors.

With such an esteem for souls and for the Precious Blood shed for them, his devotedness and success may be conceived. Not satisfied with the ordinary invitations to idolaters, he entered into their appreciation of things, and, like St. Francis Xavier, conformed to their usages; he surmounted the repugnance of nature and the most legitimate habits to become like the Apostle of the Gentiles, all things to all men, to gain them to Christ. Thus did he merit the special gift which he seems to have received from heaven for the conversion of the Japanese. His success was really prodigious, especially when we consider that precisely at this time a sort of terror overspread the country, and the missionaries themselves were obliged from prudence to moderate their proselytism. Authentic documents employed in the process for the beatification of the venerable servant of God, demonstrate that during his residence in Japan he baptized with his own hand more than five thousand idolaters. What would have been the result had he been enabled to devote himself constantly to the work of conversions, or had longer retained his pastoral functions? But he did not remain quite two years at Aria; the following years he was employed in the interior of the community.

IV.—His Domestic Offices.

As soon as Blessed Charles was familiarized with the usages of the country, and knew by his own experience the life and necessities of the religious houses in Japan, he was summoned to more delicate functions of a general interest. He had spent nearly two years at Aria, just long enough to create a lasting attachment in his flock for him, when he received orders to leave them. For ordinary men, these abrupt changes are painful trials insupportable even for some, but the holy religious was far above such weakness. Long before landing in Japan he had contracted the habit of the most simple and absolute obedience. At the first sign of his superior's will he set out for Meaco, then capital of Japan.

In this city, the centre of pagan fanaticism, under the eyes of the emperor, the Jesuits had a flourishing college, which by the number and rank of its students, and by its central position, exercised an important influence over the other houses of the Society. And how often has not the religious spirit been lost or revived in a whole order, as it rose or fell in a single house! Here, then, the principles and customs of apostolic life were to be maintained in vigor, and that at a critical moment when the slightest faults might entail such grave consequences for the future. To watch over these interests required not only a man of tried and exemplary life, but one gifted with those rare qualities which command respect as much as love. Blessed Charles Spinola was this man, and for the seven years that he held the office of minister, he fully justified the opinion conceived of his merit and virtue.

For a college of the Society of Jesus has two duties: to require of each exactness in all his duties, and furnish him all that his health and employments require. The least inclination to severity or indulgence offends or relaxes, and nothing is more difficult than to unite by a just moderation mildness with firmness, *fortiter et suaviter*. Blessed Charles succeeded to that degree that in his lifetime he was proposed as a model by his first superiors. Father Francis Pacheco, one of the most eminent missionaries of the time, urged young missionaries to maintain frequent and intimate intercourse with that fervent religious, especially in order to learn of him the practice of perfect charity. By an imperturbable goodness of heart, was the holy missionary ever distinguished in the discharge of his duties. Zealous as he was for religious discipline, he placed the care of his brethren in Christ above the duty of admonishing them; he did both with a mildness and equanimity that never varied.

He was severe only to himself. He was thus severe at all times without evincing it; but in a college, and in such a post, it was impossible to conceal from the young religious the rigors of his mortification. After the example of St. Paul, "he chastised his body to bring it into subjection." When in good health he used his discipline every night, and during Lent he prolonged this exercise to blood. He frequently wore a hair shirt, the points of which entered his flesh. He fasted on the eves of all important feasts, and his ordinary diet was a sort of perpetual fast. He had completely renounced all that can be called the delicacies of the table. He would not even touch the fruits which in that country are sought as a necessity by Europeans.[1] When at a later day he

---

[1] Saint Francis Xavier in his letters warns missionaries that in

was obliged on account of his health to take some, an order of his superiors prescribing them was necessary.

So austere a life admirably disposed him for prayer. Having broken down the obstacles raised by the senses to God's action on souls, he rose without effort and found in his union with Jesus a first reward of his sacrifice. The annual retreat was his delight. His first care was to choose a time when he was less likely to be interrupted in his communings with God: his next care to cut off vigorously during the time all external occupations: finally, if the circumstances permitted him, he prolonged his retreat beyond the eight days prescribed by the rule, and he annually made the great retreat of a month assigned by Saint Ignatius only to the years of probation. What then passed in his soul can only be conjectured from the surprising effects of his zeal and love. He came forth from these communications with God like another Moses, all penetrated with the divine Presence, and, so to speak, imbued with Jesus; and his mouth spoke from the fulness of his heart. These sentiments were maintained by the fervor of his daily meditation and all other religious acts. He there enjoyed consolations and ravishments which he in vain endeavored to conceal. During holy Mass his face was ordinarily radiant and his breast palpitated; his

---

Japan they will find no food but rice, some vegetables, and insipid, unsubstantial herbs; and that the mission requires not only men of tried and superior virtue, but also of a robust constitution, " such as Belgians and Germans," he adds.

tears streamed down abundantly. As we have seen, he drew from the true fountain, " from the Saviour's fountains," fortitude of soul and the love of suffering, of which his life furnishes continual proof. We will here cite an example where his courage served to uphold some Portuguese.

During his stay at Meaco it happened that some Japanese came to complain to the emperor of the conduct of Portuguese. In a dispute with some merchants of that nation at Macao, they had been, they said, ill treated by them and their countrymen. The emperor received the complaint, but resolved to await a favorable moment to punish the wrong done his subjects. The occasion could not fail to offer soon, on account of the commercial intercourse between Macao and Japan. The first Portuguese ship that arrived was seized; the captain and his officers were taken to the palace to undergo the punishment it might please his Japanese majesty to inflict. The least resistance, it was said, would entail the massacre of all foreigners. Matters went no further, but these arrests and threats had filled all minds with alarm; many Portuguese regarded themselves already as victims doomed to death, when the calm words of Blessed Spinola came with all their unction. He appeased the tumult and filled all hearts with the sentiment which raises the Christian above the tyrants of earth.

This incident shows us that the man of God possessed abroad the same authority that he exercised so mildly at home. All felt the influence of his zeal, and the force of circumstances gradually gave him new charges. Without neglecting his duties as minister, he had a confessional in the church, he made apostolic excursions out of the city, he directed as at Arima a very important sodality and also took a very active part in the astronomical observatory of the college. He found means to meet all, and seemed to multiply himself. He showed assiduity in the confessional and a patience that more than once excited the admiration of the public as well as of his brethren. In his excursions he was so unsparing of himself that he sometimes was in serious danger. One day he attempted to cross a river in a wretched boat, which capsized, plunging the missionary into the current. He was drawn out alive, but his health was affected and he was long subject to very painful rheumatism.

If in consequence of this malady he was less engaged abroad, he devoted himself all the more ardently to his work of predilection, the Catechists' Sodality. As its name indicates, this sodality was composed of catechists; its special object was works of mercy. It collected the alms of the more wealthy Christians, in order to relieve indigent families, take care of the sick and save little children, there as in China exposed on the river side by idolatrous parents. As is evident, such a sodality contained in embryo the great charitable institutions that constitute the glory of the nineteenth century: The Society of St. Vincent de Paul, the Association for the Propagation of the Faith, with that of the Holy Infancy. To the catechists, these useful auxiliaries to missionaries, it proved a school of sanctity and a continual exercise of apostolic zeal.

The direction of these men afforded Blessed Charles a precious opportunity of displaying all the resources of his talent and devotedness. In works of charity, he did not merely exhort, but he also readily contributed in person, not only by begging from door to door, but by carrying, on his own shoulders, the various objects he received. Thus laden, he would visit the poor and miserable, and with the nourishment of the body administer the much more precious spiritual aliment of the word of God. He neglected no one; if he showed any preference, it was for the more miserable and disgusting objects of charity. In these visits, joy beamed on his comely visage. The nobleness of his origin betrayed itself in the appearance of him become as a menial for the love of Christ; and all he did for his own humiliation served but to excite the most profound veneration for him wherever he went.

This sentiment of veneration was more general even among the higher orders. In their eyes the science of the holy missionary equalled his sanctity; and no sermon was more efficacious for them than to behold the same man pass from the lowly hovel of the poor to the observatory of the professor. Herein our Blessed, who excelled in this latter department, explained to them the various celestial phenomena, and his lessons were received with admiration.[1]

---

[1] The Jesuits' observatories in Japan were not simply means of

We may then easily conceive how great must have been the astonishment and the painful emotions which agitated the faithful of Meaco, when the news of his approaching departure was announced. During the seven years which they had the happiness of possessing him, they had considered him as the necessary man, the indispensable instrument of God's Providence towards them. But the same reasons which called him from Aria to Meaco caused him to pass from this latter city to Nagasaki, there to discharge the duties of Procurator-General of the whole Japanese mission.

The Procurator is entrusted with the administration of the temporal affairs, that is to say, of the human means of existence. This office, everywhere of great importance for the stability of apostolic undertakings, was moreover, in Japan, of a very difficult and delicate nature. No establishment owned anything as its own: there was a common fund, whence the procurator endeavored to provide for all the wants of the mission. But how often was he not obliged to see the most necessary supplies delayed! What charity on the one hand, and what confidence on the other, in order that the distribution of supplies should give

conversion among an inquiring and intelligent nation; they were also means of scientific progress. Blessed Charles Spinola, in this respect, rendered real services, which are mentioned in our European records. Witness the following, which I owe to the kindness of Father Aug. De Backer:

Observation of a lunar eclipse, by Rev. Father Charles Spinola, at Nagasaki in 1612, and inserted in the Memoirs of the Academy of Sciences, vol. 7, page 706.

rise to no complaints, no murmurs. Once more, it was far more the virtue of our Blessed, than his well established abilities, which caused him to be named to this office, precisely at the moment when the persecution was about to render life more painful and resources more scanty. The difficulties and the dangers of the post were too visible and too serious not to affect him : he understood and received them with the calm courage which characterized his great soul : but he could not refrain from sentiments of deep sensibility at the sight of the scenes of attachment and of regret, which marked his farewell to the Christians of Meaco. His catechists especially, disconsolate at the loss of their kind Father, seemed unable to part with him—they escorted him a considerable distance from the city, and then bathed in tears received his last instructions and directions, asserting their inviolable fidelity to the faith of Christ. The sequel proved their sincerity.

Nagasaki, the commercial metropolis of Japan, was naturally designed to be the residence of the Procurator-General of the Mission. He remained there seven years, discharging the duties to the satisfaction of his brethren in the Apostleship, up to the moment he was cast into the horrible prison of which we are soon to speak. From the commencement of his administration, he was obliged to conceal himself from the pursuit of the tyrant, and it was only through the greatest efforts that he could then procure even slender means for the persecuted missionaries. But it is time to give an account of this persecution which for two centuries and a half has oppressed the finest portion of the Oriental Church.

V.—THE GREAT PERSECUTION.

No persecution has ever produced more disastrous results than that excited against the Christians of Japan by the Emperor Daifu-Sama. There as every where else, it may be truly said that the blood of martyrs is the seed of Christians; but the infernal plan was so ably combined, the torments so horribly prolonged, the searches so thorough, that finally, after thirty years slaughter, not a victim was left, not a Christian was to be found, not a trace of Christianity remained. Did the Faith still reserve to itself a last asylum in the depths of consciences and in the secrecy of the domestic sanctuary? We can suppose so, and the future will perhaps produce the proof.[1] Whatever it be, let us give in a few words the leading facts of this persecution unparalleled in the annals of the world.

The Church in Japan, after sixty-two years of existence, contained in 1612 nearly two millions of Catholics. The number of missionaries, not including the Japanese priests and the Catechists, was one hundred and fifty, all religious: nine Dominicans, fourteen

---

[1] Since the above was written, most interesting news has been received from Japan, which shows that, by a prodigy of God's grace, large numbers of Christians are still to be found in that land of persecution. In the introduction we have given, extracts may be seen from the Annals of the Propagation of the Faith for March 1869.

Franciscans, four Augustinians, and one hundred and twenty-three Jesuits. The latter had possessed one hundred and sixty houses, but forced to bend to the violence of the storm, they possessed at the moment only thirty colleges or residences. This prosperous state was much enhanced by the excellent dispositions of the Christians themselves. The noble qualities of the Japanese were very favorable to religion; they had become, under the action of divine grace, heroic virtues, which, even in the weaker sex and in the tenderest age, we shall see raising them superior to the most cruel tortures.

Daifu-Sama, as we had remarked, had begun his career by suspending all persecution against the Christians, and he continued to follow this course until 1612. At this time, the most perfidious influences combined to produce a great change in his mind. The rapid diffusion of Christianity in his dominions of itself presented nothing alarming to the monarch, but his pagan courtiers, jealous of the favor of their master, were afraid of being supplanted. They revived the suspicions which had already proved so successful with Taico-Sama:

"Was it likely that men learned and prudent, as, beyond all doubt, these Europeans were, would have abandoned their country, traversed the seas, endured numberless hardships, with the sole view of benefiting strangers, without consulting their own self-interest? No, no; religion served them as a pretext: it covered the design of conquering Japan, as it had served to subject the Philippines to the King of Spain."

These repeated insinuations caused the emperor to reflect on this matter; they disposed him to interpret unfavorably acts of some Europeans which were, of themselves, most indifferent. A Spanish ambassador arrived in Japan upon one of those enormous vessels which the vanity of the Castillians willingly displayed; the pilot, on approaching land, fearing to strike on reefs where several vessels had been already lost, advanced slowly and cautiously, sounding as he went.

"What does this mean?" murmur the Japanese; "why this minute exploration?"

"Why?" replies some ill-disposed Protestant; "among Europeans the question would be quickly solved."

"How so?"

"The manner in which the Spaniards have acted would be considered as an insult and a sort of declaration of war; moreover, it is plain enough, the conquest of Japan is half accomplished; the missionaries have done the work; their action is more certain and efficient than that of an army."

Candid explanations might, perhaps, yet have prevented the effect of this excitement and brought the Emperor back to friendly dispositions, but the commercial interests of the Europeans had suggested to them a new source of profit. For a long time, the English and Hollanders had everywhere followed in the track of the Portuguese and Spaniards. They were especially jealous of the privileges which the commerce of these nations enjoyed in the far East. This jealousy was further embittered by religious prejudice. In England, as well as in Holland, the government was bitterly hostile to Catholics and pursued them by persecuting laws. The merchants and rovers carried the popular prejudice to the ends of the earth. They distorted everything to injure the Catholic nations. An idolatrous emperor, suspicious of all foreigners, was easily persuaded.

Daifu-Sama's mind being thus poisoned by their representations, the Christian religion was thenceforward in his eyes nothing but a treacherous device made use of by the King of Spain; and the Jesuits but political emissaries, whom several of the governments had for similar reasons banished their country. "What is there to prevent me from doing the same?" one day inquired the Emperor. And he at once wrote to the King of Arima, and renewed an ancient edict which prohibited any noble or soldier to profess the Christian religion.

This measure showed the policy of the deceived monarch; while he thus branded Christianity as a disgrace to nobility and to the profession of arms, he wished to prepare defenders against foreigners. If he expected to cause the Christian officers of his court to apostatize, he was disappointed. These worthy servants of God declared unanimously that while they obeyed the emperor in all things else, they remained resolute on this point. Such was also the answer of the nobles and of the soldiers in the provinces, and four hundred of them suffered, with constancy, confiscation of their property and exile. In the kingdom of Arima, all of whom were Christian, the persecution immediately assumed a more violent character. Michael Suquendono, an apostate, reigned there, having reached the throne by fratricide. Through ambition, he repudiated his lawful wife, in order to espouse the niece of the emperor. His chief counsellor was an audacious man named Suffioye, governor of Nagasaki. At his instigation, Suquendono had recourse to degrading punishments against the Christians—to proscription, to means of destruction and punishments hitherto unknown in Japan. On the 6th of October, 1613, he caused eight of the first nobility of the city of Arima to be burned to death.

Twenty thousand Christians assembled to witness the execution or rather the triumph of their brethren. They formed in procession and moved on in great order with the martyrs, reciting prayers and chanting hymns. Arrived at the place of punishment, they stood in ranks around the funeral piles, as if to offer to God the first fruits of this glorious community. I cannot forbear inserting here two incidents related by Father de Charlevoix in his History of Japan.

Among these martyrs were James Mundo, a boy of twelve, with his sister Magdalen, aged twenty, and their mother.

The cords which attached the boy being burnt, he ran through the flames to embrace his mother and die in her arms; not escape, as some thought at first.

"My son," exclaimed this incomparable woman, "My son, look up to heaven; say: Jesus, Mary!" The poor boy, repeated thrice: "Jesus, Mary!" and fell; the mother, at the same moment, sank upon him, and they expired together.

The daughter of this heroine presented a spectacle still more surprising. She alone still remained erect, and though enveloped in flames she appeared full of life and vigor. On beholding her thus immovable, with her eyes sweetly raised towards heaven, one would have said she was quite insensible; on a sudden, however, it was noticed that she was gathering burning coals, which she placed upon her head in form of a crown. She seemed thus to deck herself before going to meet her divine Spouse. She then sank down the stake, reclined upon the couch of fire and expired.[1]

When the news of this imposing demonstration reached the emperor, it produced upon his mind an effect which the enemies of Christianity did not fail to turn to their own advantage.

"To what could not the audacity of such men be led?" "What blind devotedness to a crucified man! What contempt for the gods of the country, and for the orders of the emperor! Would it not be necessary to exterminate this sect even to the last vestige, and at any cost?"

---

[1] The relics of these martyrs were collected, and a brief of Urban VIII., to the Carmelites of Florence, mentions "the bone of the hand of the *Blessed* Mary Magdalen, a Japanese virgin, who had suffered martyrdom by fire for the faith of Jesus Christ."

These suggestions had their effect. On 19th February, 1614, the decree was published at Meaco and sent to all the kingdoms of Japan which *obliged all the missionaries to proceed to Nagasaki within seven days, and to embark for their own country without delay.* The most severe penalties were pronounced against all who harbored them.

The order was too formal, this time, to be eluded entirely. Prudence, therefore, suggested prompt submission. The missionaries gave their last instructions to the faithful how to act during the persecution, and with intense bitterness of grief but with equal firmness on the part of both, they were obliged to part with the children whom they had begotten in Christ. Some, and by far the greater number, went into exile, the rest concealed themselves to minister to the Christians.

The persecution, opened in this decisive way, pursued its course. Churches were demolished, all external signs of Catholic worship suppressed, and on the 26th of February, only four days after the departure of the missionaries, the streets of Meaco re-echoed the sweeping proscription: " Whoever does not abjure the Christian religion shall be burnt alive." "The rebels," added the herald, "have only to prepare their own stakes." Serious or in jest, these words produced an unexpected effect: the next day all the streets of the city were lined with stakes, each Christian wishing to evince his eagerness to die for his religion. Before such a manifestation the emperor recoiled, and at first merely banished to the north the heads of the highest families. Then the deportation became more general. Before the close of the year two convoys set sail, one for Macao, the other for the Philippines. They comprised illustrious laymen, such as Justo Ucondono,[1] with his family, ninety-six Jesuits, several other religious of various orders, and a great number of catechists, in all fifteen hundred persons—the flower of the Japanese Church. Several of these missionaries subsequently entered Japan in various disguises, and many others were allured by the hope of gaining the martyr's crown.

The civil war between Daifu-Sama and the son of Taico gave the faithful a short respite. After a bloody battle, Taico's son, besieged in the castle of Osaca, preferred to die amid the flames, rather than surrender to his former guardian. The latter did not long enjoy his victory; he died in March, 1616, leaving the the throne to his son, Xongun, and to his descendants, who have, till so recent a date, retained it. He at the same time bequeathed to them his hatred of Christianity. The fire of persecution was rekindled throughout the empire, and ravaged especially the congregations of the faithful in the islands of Firando and Ximo, nor was it to cease till there were no more victims. Till then it was a gigantic struggle between the tyrants and the faithful; the former incessantly inventing tortures, more and more atrocious, the latter

---

[1] This illustrious confessor of Christ died at Manilla in the odor of sanctity.

seeming to draw new energy from the very refinements of cruelty. They were torn with pincers, their bodies gashed all over, their necks slowly sawed; they were roasted for several hours; means were discovered to keep them alive for days, hung up by the feet with their heads in a pit: nothing shook their constancy. Even at the stake they blessed, exhorted, chanted the praises of God. Thus died in the outset of the persecution thousands of Christians, and, by a touching disposition of divine Providence, the acts of their martyrdom were collected and sent to Rome by Blessed Charles Spinola. Thus what he had formerly done from devotion, he now did as a duty, and with the authority conferred by his title of Vicar-General for the Southern part of the Empire. While awaiting till it should be given him to share the glory of the martyrs, he celebrated it, and prepared for it by the labors we are now to describe.

VI.—Secret Missions of Blessed Charles Spinola.

The missionaries had disappeared with all outward signs of Christian worship, but they had not all left Japan. The post was dangerous, and, for this reason, sought by all these valiant soldiers of Christ. Each in emulation put forward his claims. The bishop having just died, the clergy elected as vicar-general Father de Carvajal, provincial of the Jesuits. It was hard for a pastor to leave his flock at such a moment, but banished by name, and, moreover, too well known to elude the pursuit directed against him, he could not remain in Japan without compromising with himself the whole church. The procurator-general was naturally the one to replace him; as a precious grace he asked permission to remain with the persecuted faithful, basing his request on the duties of his office. He could not but be accepted. They were too happy to retain at the head of the Christian body a man of so much experience and tried prudence. Our saint was accordingly appointed with twenty-two Fathers of the Society and several other religious to attend to the interests of the mission during the persecution.

At this intelligence the holy missionary, habitually calm and reserved, could not refrain from expressions of joy. In the decision arrived at by his superior, he beheld a sure pledge of the martyrdom which awaited him; he now regarded the office previously imposed upon him as a means intended by God for this object; he recalled with admiration the constant ways of Providence over him, and revelled in the sentiment of happiness. "This feeling is such," he wrote to a Father in Europe, "that it even surpasses the joy I experienced on being sent to Japan."

Meanwhile, Suffioye, governor of Nagasaki, prepared to execute the emperor's orders vigorously; he framed his plans especially to prevent any religious from finding an asylum in the city confided to his administration. The customs of Japan facilitated the organization of his police. In that country all the streets have barriers closed at nightfall, and each quarter has its commissary to watch over its inhabitants. The governor commanded each of these, under penalty of confiscation and death, not to permit any religious to remain in his district. These orders, with the penalties pronounced against harborers, rendered the position of the missionaries very difficult and delicate. But Christian charity was not to be overcome by the world's hatred; only it has recourse, for religion's own interests, to all the precautions prudence could suggest. Blessed Charles Spinola, like most of the missionaries, felt obliged to use these precautions. He desired martyrdom, but he would not hasten to the executioner. He feared to destroy his mission or advance the hour appointed by the Sovereign Master of Life. While awaiting this hour, he devoted himself, with a noble heart, to the afflicted church and the Christians persecuted for the faith.

With this view he began by changing his name, and to show the secret desire of his soul, called himself Joseph of the Cross. But he could not as easily change his countenance; disguise himself as he might, he could not appear in public without being instantly recognized as a European. He was accordingly obliged to keep shut up by day, and to invent a thousand devices to deceive the police at night. He was incessantly obliged to change his hiding-place so as to baffle pursuit; all the Christian houses were open to him, but he could enter none without exposing his best friends, or himself to be betrayed by some false brother. This last danger filled his painful position with bitterness. A few unhappy men, who in the violent tortures had apostatized gave rise to distrust, and necessarily diminished mutual intercourse. The police, on their side, aware of the Father's presence, increased their rigor and vigilance, and of course paid treachery well. How was it possible to escape so many snares without a special protection of God? He could not be hid and merely seek to save his own life; amid spies and informers ever on the alert, living from day to day without any resource, he had nevertheless the duty of pastor and apostle to fulfil; baptize children, administer to the dying, hear confessions, confer the other sacraments, celebrate mass, more than once even on Sundays; support the weak, restrain the rash, devote himself to all the increasing wants. Yet our Blessed Charles led this life for four years. He thus speaks of it himself, with habitual modesty, in a letter dated March 20, 1617, and addressed to Father Lambertengo, at Milan:

"For nearly two years and a half I have devoted myself to encourage and support the Christians of this country, not without great difficulty. Having no home, I pass secretly from house to house, to hear confessions and celebrate our holy mysteries by night. Most of my time I spend in utter solitude, deprived of all human converse and consolation, having only that which God gives to those who suffer for his love. What affects me most is, to see the ravages committed in the vineyard of the Lord; not only the branches and the budding fruit torn by the wind of persecution, but the grapes, whose approaching maturity was about to reward us for so many souls. However I am tolerably well, and, though destitute of almost everything and taking but one scanty meal a day, I do not fall away. Does not this prove that "man liveth not by bread alone?"

Meanwhile the great consolation which the holy missionary promised himself in this painful ministry seemed to flee him; he escaped all pursuit, and moreover the rumor ran that the Japanese authorities had ceased putting foreign priests to death. But his anxiety on this point was not of long duration. On the 22d of May, 1617, the emperor Xongun put to death two missionaries, Father J. B. Machado, a Jesuit, and Father Peter of the Assumption, a Franciscan, both of the number of martyrs beatified by Pius IX. on the 7th of July, 1867. At this event Blessed Charles felt all his dearest hopes suddenly revive, as he was nearly captured himself. He needed to pour out his soul, as he did in a letter written on the 5th of October to the General, Father Mutius Vitelleschi. We extract the following passage:

"How happy I deem myself to have remained here to witness so glorious a triumph! I should have obtained the same favor, I have no doubt, had I not been confined to my room by erysipelas for two months. If I had then, as I had proposed, been able to visit the two Christian districts confided to my care, I should doubtless have been discovered and taken by the soldiers of Omura. My sins have deprived me of this noble crown, and I feel all my own unworthiness. Still to judge by what I see, the grace is but deferred, not lost. Awaiting it, I devote myself entirely to the Christians, whom I exhort to face martyrdom courageously, holding myself ever in readiness to lay down my life for Him who so generously sacrificed his for me. As my duty of procurator prevents my keeping myself as carefully concealed as the other Fathers, who have occasion to apply to me, I expect to be the first to undergo imprisonment and death."

The last phrase of the letter confirms what has been already said of his sentiments in regard to the duties of his office. He clings to it in hopes of martyrdom, as indeed he did to all the perilous functions of the holy ministry. He could not be accused of rashness; he neglected no reasonable precaution: but when requisite he strode through the midst of dangers with perfect serenity and a holy eagerness to consummate his sacrifice. In this disposition he pursued his secret apostleship till the day of his arrest.

The emperor Xongun, worthy son of Daifu, was deeply incensed to learn not only that some missionaries still remained in Japan, but their number had even been increased. By his order Gonroc, the new governor of Nagasaki, used every means to entrap them. He adroitly spread the report that the new governor was opposed to useless vexations; that he would indeed watch all going around at night, but that he did not intend to harass the people by domiciliary visits. These rumors were too encouraging to excite confidence, and Blessed Charles Spinola, instead of becoming less guarded, redoubled his precautions. Hid in the most secret apartments, he came forth only to confess the sick, or when ordered by the Father Visitor; he even for a time abstained entirely from exercising the holy ministry. He appeared thus more secure than ever, when God visited him with a malady which required him to leave his place of retreat in order to be treated in a house better located. He took up his residence with a poor Portuguese named Dominic Giorgi, and refrained from all intercourse with persons abroad.

Whether he had at this time some premonitory revelation of his approaching martyrdom, as some have thought, it is impossible to say. He certainly had a presentiment. During the last month of his liberty, all noticed in him an extraordinary increase of fervor. He devoted more time to prayer, he celebrated Mass with greater devotion and in a sort of ecstacy; his conversation was more than usually marked by a holy joy and a sweet affability. His accounts had always been well kept. He revised them, and confided the books with explanatory notes to another Father. Two days before his arrest, on leaving his habitual meditation, he called his catechist, and, like a man making all his last arrangements, gave him some articles to conceal in a secure place, and some pictures to distribute to his friends after his death. Then taking two rosaries, "Give one," he said, "to your sister, the other to your younger brother." He had now left only a small Japanese hat, which he offered his catechist. The latter declined, saying he did not need it. "Keep it," said the Father, "to remember me." "Ah!

Father," said the affected catechist, " I need nothing to remind me of you : you have done too much for me ever to forget you, and besides I will never survive you. I will cling so to you that they shall not put you to death without killing me." " As for me," said the holy man, " what God wills will happen to me ; but for you, you shall not be harmed." The event justified his words.

The preceding details have been transmitted to us by eye-witnesses ; what follows is drawn chiefly from a letter written to the Rector of the College of Milan by Father Spinola himself, from the prison at Omura, March 3, 1619.

The house of the Portuguese seemed no longer to afford a secure shelter, and Father Spinola resolved to withdraw to some other. He was to make this change on the eve of the feast of St. Lucy, December 13, 1618, when he received a visit from a missionary. On the other hand, his host's wife, Elizabeth Fernandez, wishing to receive communion on the following morning, begged of him to grant her this last consolation ; even his friends, far from hastening his departure, advised him to wait, as it would afford a few more hours to provide for a new retreat ; the Father was to say mass before daybreak, and remain carefully concealed until the very moment of his departure. Such were the designs of man, but Divine Providence had another fate in store for him.

Father Spinola had retired to bed and was sleeping. Towards midnight he thought he heard thieves breaking the doors and making their way into the house; it was only a dream: having found that his alarms were groundless, he tried in vain to sleep again. Scarcely half an hour after, Gouroc's soldiers really appeared. They forced an entrance and immediately rushed to the bedchamber of Brother Ambrose Fernandez. They seized him, as well as the master of the house, hurried them off, and when on the point of leaving, as they passed a second time before Father Spinola's room, one of them opened the door and discovered him. The holy man had heard everything, and from the first moment had betaken himself to prayer, leaving his fate in the hands of Divine Providence. Seeing that he was discovered, he raised his eyes and hands towards heaven, and in a burst of unutterable joy, humbly thanked God.

PART IV.

MARTYRDOM.

1.—The Examination.

Henceforth we shall follow our holy Apostle on the sorrowful way, which, marked at every step by suffering, will lead him at last to the stake. It is martyrdom in all its horror, or to speak more correctly, with all its sublimity. Such an end could, if need be, atone for the most culpable wickedness; it is in short an act of unbounded love; Jesus has said it, and the Church proposes it; as soon as she has established the fact of martyrdom, she closes the process of canonization, she bows before him whom God crowns in heaven, and invites the faithful to do likewise. If this holds good for every case of martyrdom, what shall we say concerning the sublime death of Father Spinola, which closed the holy career we have thus traced? What shall we say of a four years' martyrdom, endured with the most heroic constancy? But let us come to facts and gather with respect the most trifling particulars.

Father Spinola had been discovered amidst the shouts of the soldiers. In their eyes he was the head of the Christians. What a victim! They fell upon him, put a rope around his neck, bound his hands and feet, and so cruelly did the ropes leave their marks deep in his flesh, that he bore them for the rest of his life. In this state he was dragged off with Brother Fernandez and his Portuguese host before the governor, where shortly after two Dominican Fathers arrived. That day and the following night they passed together in a barnyard near a stable, exposed to all the rigor of the seasons. Whilst there, some Christian servants of the governor slackened the bonds of our martyr, and he spent the night in hearing their confessions. Whilst there also, the four religious obtained and put on their habits.

The following morning Gonroc summoned them before him, and after asking them their name, age, and their country, spoke as follows, addressing Father Spinola:

"I do not understand your conduct; you come here, as you claim, to give life to the Japanese; but you do quite the contrary; many Japanese lose their lives on your account." He evidently knew nothing or pretended to know nothing of the first elements of the question. The Father took advantage of this opportunity to teach him some salutary truths. He spoke as follows:

"This mortal life, my lord, and everything dependent on it, swiftly pass away; we must one day leave them all. What is of deep moment to all and deserves all our care is our soul, which is immortal. Since then the welfare of the soul depends on our keeping the Law of Christ, what wonder if the Japanese who have understood this truth show their joy at obtaining life everlasting, at the cost of a slight sacrifice, the sacrifice of this miserable temporary existence. For my part, I have for many years sighed after this happy moment; and since, thanks to you, I have arrived at the consummation of my wishes, I am filled with gratitude. Far from complaining of the emperor or his ministers, I beg of God with my whole heart to reward them, by granting them the knowledge of the truth, and leading them in the path of salvation."

The governor of course had nothing to say in reply, for he abruptly left to dine. After dinner he summoned Father Spinola alone; the latter was brought to a private room, where the governor and two friends were waiting for him. Then Gonroc made him undergo a searching and insidious examination, which resulted in nothing except in making manifest the missionary's presence of mind, or rather, the divine help, which our Lord has promised to those who will confess his faith in similar circumstances.

" How came you to take up your abode in Japan," asked the governor, " and in what houses did you conceal yourself?"

" Christians," replied the Father, " have a thousand ways of escaping the vigilance of their enemies; but I cannot make them known, nor betray the friends, who have harbored me."

" If you are so delicate regarding your friends, why did you expose them to death by hiding yourself in their houses?"

"I have never intended to hurt any person. If I have enjoyed the hospitality of any Japanese, it is because they had invited me for the good of their souls; moreover, I first exposed myself for their sake."

"But if the emperor does not wish your presence in his dominions, why do you obstinately remain here, in spite of his prohibition?"

"Permit me, my lord, to ask a question in my turn. If a king of Japan gave you a command, and Xongun, lord of all the kings of Japan, ordered you to do the contrary, which of the two would you obey? Would you not do the will of the emperor and justify your conduct before his inferior? Such is my position; I do all in my power to show my respect for the emperor. Although I am a religious, I do not wear the habit of my order; I do not preach in public; I conceal myself and perform the duties of my office in darkness and at night. But since the Lord of-heaven and earth, the King of kings, commands me to continue in the discharge of my ministry, I think it my duty to obey his sovereign will, even at the risk of my life."

"Ingenious sophism," exclaimed the governor, turning to his friends.

"My lord," replied Spinola, "this is no sophism, it is an eternal, unchangeable law, which we cannot alter; much less is it a scheme to obtain possession of your countries and your empire, as some persons think. If this were so, we could have brought you a religion less severe and more pleasing to the great ones of the earth than our religion is ; we would have preached a law flattering to the senses ; and we would not, as you yourselves own we do, abstain from carnal pleasures, or at least we would act as your Bonzes—combine outward austerity with secret indulgence."

The bold apostle, receiving no answer, continued to expose the follies of the Japanese worship, until Gonroc bade his friends call the two Dominican Fathers. Father Spinola remained to act as interpreter. Being alone with his judge, he took advantage of the opportunity to speak to him concerning the kingdom of God and to exhort him to become a Christian.

"You are too enlightened, my lord," said he to the governor, "to die in such a faith as yours; for I do not charge upon you the cruel treatment inflicted on me; you fulfil the commands of others. Be instructed in a more perfect Law than that of your Bonzes and idols. My zeal for your welfare urges me to speak thus to you."

Gonroc smiled at these words, and having ascertained that no one was near enough to hear him, he answered that the Christian religion did not please him.

"You do not love it, because you know it not," answered our apostle; "receive instruction and you will like it."

Here he was interrupted by the arrival of the other prisoners, and never had an opportunity to renew his conversation with the governor. The generous attempt of the saint proved without avail; for it is difficult to convert men whose wickedness is the offspring of ambition.

The examination of the Dominican Father was marked only by the apostolic intrepidity with which Father Spinola defended the missionaries. When asked when and from what vessel they had landed in Japan, they answered through Father Spinola, "that they had left the Philippines a few months before;" but they refused to give the name of the owner of the ship in which they had come, fearing that it might cost him his life.

"You would do much better," said the governor, sharply, "to stay at home and work out your own salvation without troubling us." This taunt again changed the interpreter into the apostle:

"Priests harm nobody," said he; "they only go whither they are called. We know that many prefer their property to their soul, and that they think little of missionaries. But there are more who aspire to heavenly favors, and who receive us in their houses at the risk of their lives. Imprisonment, nay, death itself, undergone for their faith, crowns the happiness of these generous Christians. At their urgent prayers we have remained; their sufferings, therefore, cannot be imputed to us. True, we cheerfully acceded to their request. The zealous Christian is not satisfied with insuring his own salvation; charity is a fire which spreads and tends to kindle the whole world. Seeing you enveloped in the darkness of error, missionaries leave their homes, brave the fury of the ocean and come to die in Japan, in order to convey to you the light of the true faith and the treasure of everlasting life."

These words are but a feeble sketch of the discourse delivered by Father Spinola on this occasion. "Never, as he owned, had he felt himself stirred to speak with such eloquence; and never had he spoken Japanese with so much ease; he referred the glory to Him who fights and triumphs in his servants.

During this examination, an officer from Omura, for whom Gonroc had sent, to take charge of the missionaries, arrived. He intended to keep the Japanese prisoners at Nagasaki, but the presence of the Fathers in a city filled with Christians would have caused too great a sensation. For this reason he sent them to Omura, where the Dominican Father Thomas of the Holy Ghost, and Father Apollinaris, a Franciscan, were already confined with six native Christians.

When it became known at Nagasaki that the prisoners were to be sent to Omura, the people crowded the streets through which the Confessors were to pass, and the throng was so dense that the officer refused to take the responsibility of escorting them; he waited for them on the opposite shore of the bay; Gonroc's soldiers conveyed them to that point. They passed through some streets of Nagasaki amid the sobs and tears of the faithful, whom the guards could not prevent from approaching the martyrs, to bid them farewell and reverently touch their habits.

Father Spinola would gladly have addressed them

some words of encouragement, but time was not allowed to him. They wished to escape the crowd and embark. As he departed our Saint could not banish the wretched Gonroc from his thoughts. Wishing to give him a last token of his interest, he begged the captain of the escort to salute him from him, and assure him that "he entertained only the kindest sentiments towards him."

After a short passage over, the prisoners reached Uraca, where the Omura officer awaited them with horses and a good escort. This officer showed great civility; he even apologized to Father Spinola for the duties he was unwillingly obliged to perform, at the same time unbinding his hands and giving him a good horse. On the road to Omura the prisoners sang psalms or meditated on the captivity of our Lord, rejoicing like the apostles "to have been found worthy to suffer for Jesus Christ."

Blessed Charles Spinola, ever attentive to the good of souls, availed himself of a halt at night to hear the confessions of some Christians; for all the roads were full of them. The next day, which was a Sunday, the officer, at the moment of resuming the march, had a horse brought for Father Spinola; but he preferred to travel on foot the short distance that led to the spot where he was to embark for his prison. They embarked, and soon perceived the sombre building that was to be the bourn of their voyage.

14

II.—THE PRISON.

On a rock jutting out into the sea near a place called Suzuta, there rose a thatched cabin. It was forty palms in length by twenty in width, that is to say, a little less than five yards by ten. The hill presented a pleasing aspect from the freshness of the verdure, but surrounded on three sides by the sea, it was exposed to all the violence of the winds and tempests. The cabin had suffered considerably, especially in the roof; it was no longer a shelter, but an enclosure, and this enclosure was to be the prison.

As soon as the three missionaries perceived their prison, they intoned the Te Deum; this chant of thanksgiving was answered by two priestly voices; and the choir formed of those advancing to captivity and of those already subjected to its bitterness, ended at the moment when they were able to give each other the kiss of peace. Such an entrance into prison corresponded perfectly to the dispositions of our saint. "I seemed to enter a heavenly paradise," he wrote to the Rector of the College of Milan. Seized with a holy respect at the sight of those who had preceded him, he recalled the words pronounced by Pope Saint Clement on a similar occasion : " It is not by my merits," said he, " that God has sent me hither, to be a partaker of your crowns." His heart overflowed with joy. He could not be sated with the thought of his joy. "Prisoner for the faith of Jesus Christ." After the example of St. Paul, he took no other title till he could substitute that of "Condemned to death for Jesus Christ." His letters from his prison, many of which are still extant, invariably bear this signature : " Carolus incarceratus pro Fide Christi," and later, " Carolus morte damnatus pro Christiana Fide."

Under the impression of this thought, or rather under the influence of this great grace, it is easy to conceive what must have been the first effusions of the glorious prisoner. In February, 1619, he wrote to Father John Baptist Porro : " Here I am at last in prison. I was led bound like a robber through several streets of Nagasaki to the seashore, and the whole city gathered to the spectacle. I feel very happy, unable to thank God sufficiently for the favor he has granted me. Reverend Father, unite, I beg, your thanksgiving to mine, and obtain for me the end, which you know has been for so many years the object of all my desires. Since we lived together at Milan, you know my imperfections, pray God to pardon them. If my sins are the obstacle to my shedding my blood for my God, I have at least the consolation of having been found worthy to suffer opprobrium for the name of Jesus ; and this is surely no slight favor. Be his holy will accomplished in me : I ask no other consolation."

To another Father, who was at Macao, he described the ardor that animated him :

"Whereby, my God, have I merited the signal favor of suffering this opprobrium for the name of Jesus? How I bless the benign Providence that has brought me from Italy to Japan ! How well employed I deem my labors, and my sufferings well rewarded, even should I fail to win the crown I came here to seek." Constantly the same panting for martyrdom. Whatever might be his sufferings at the time, while blessing God for this first grace, he offers himself with unshaken constancy to suffer more and consummate the sacrifice. In the fervor of the first days this disposition might appear less astonishing; but it never diminished during that long torture of a noisome prison, that slow martyrdom of four years. To appreciate this heroism, it is necessary to know the condition of the prison and the life led by the martyrs.

I will say no more of the cabin in which they were at first confined. This old shell, ruinous as it was, still afforded some resource; and the prisoners under the eye of their guards were allowed to walk in the enclosure. But this state of things did not last long. The edifice threatened to fall, and it was resolved to rebuild it entirely. They began by removing the captives. On the 21st of July, 1619, they were all embarked and carried to Cubara, a place not far from Omura. They now numbered sixteen, and had only a small cabin to hold them. There nothing shielded them from the scorching rays of a July sun; no breath of wind came to refresh or purify the air they breathed, the only window in the cabin not opening even on the windward side. Their food was as wretched as their lodging. And yet, in this position, "we were gay and content," wrote our Saint to the Father General; "we thanked God for deeming us worthy to suffer for his name. But this superhuman courage did not protect them from disease. Dysentery broke out; and all would have died had they been confined in their temporary prison a few weeks longer. But after the lapse of eighteen days, as the Saint states, the new prison was completed, and the prisoners removed to it on the 7th of August, 1619.

The installation called forth new demonstrations of joy from the martyrs. They arrived singing psalms and hymns adapted to their circumstances. "I rejoiced in the things that were said to me, we shall go into the house of the Lord." They had ascertained that the new habitation would be more inconvenient than the former one: the moment they entered they saw how true it was, and our Saint addressing the guards, said: "It is very small, but I shall have all the larger abode in heaven. I pity you, poor unfortunate men, who, living in ignorance and forgetfulness of God, can expect only an eternal captivity." He then knelt on the threshold of his prison, and rising resumed the sacred chant with his companions: "Here is my rest forever: here will I abide, for I have chosen it." Let us, too, in spirit penetrate into that abode: let us lay aside all false delicacy and endeavor to bear at least the idea of what these noble martyrs endured with heroic constancy.

The plan of the prison has been traced by Blessed Spinola with accompanying explanations. (See following page.) The old prison was twenty palms by forty; the new one, it is not known by whose order,

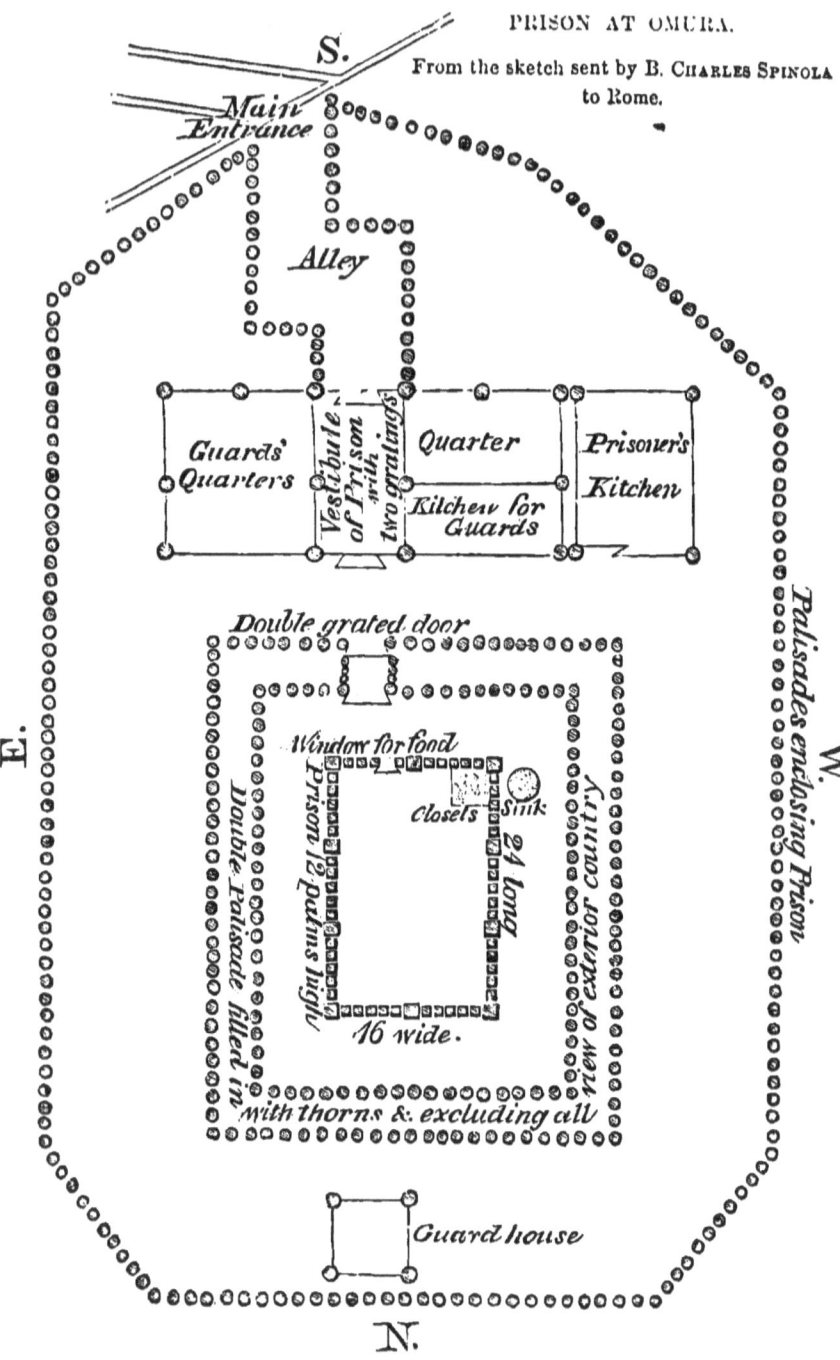

was only twenty-four by sixteen, say four yards by six.[1] It was a refinement of cruelty ; for the persecution continued to gather in its victims and heap prisoner on prisoner, and at one moment this space of less than twenty-four square yards held no less than thirty-three persons. But to comprehend the horror of this situation we must enter into further details.

This wretched den had, properly speaking, neither walls nor roof. It was a kind of pen, the bars of which were large square posts fifteen feet high, two fingers apart, and united by crosspieces.

There was a small window through which food was passed, and a very narrow door only to be used on great occasions. The prisoners never left their pen even in time of sickness, and our saint left it but twice, once to go to Firando, as we shall see, and the second time, to march to the stake. If space and materials were contracted in building the interior of the prison, they were lavished in the rest of the enclosure to multiply precautions. On the plan will be seen the three rows of palisades, with the walk around and the quarters of the guards. An officer saw to the strict observance of the regulations, and at the least sign of indulgence the guards were changed.

---

[1] B. Richard of St. Anne, in a letter published in the Revue Catholique of Louvain for May, 1867, seems to make it 24 by 16 feet instead of palms ; but if the translation be correct, the holy man mentions it merely incidentally, and cannot be supposed to be as accurate as B. Spinola in giving a careful plan of the prison.

What our martyrs had to endure in this prison surpasses all that can be imagined. Our Saint so eager for suffering and so reserved on this point, nevertheless writing to his Father General goes so far as to say: "I can assure your Reverence, that there is not one among us who, consulting only the cry of nature, would not prefer burning alive to life in this dungeon. . . . Every sense here finds a torture of its own." And, in fact, the space was allotted off so that they could not stretch out and could scarcely move; much less could they for a moment withdraw from the sight of their companions. The palisade around gave passage to the sun, the winds, and all the inclemencies of the season. During summer the heat was such that our Saint was, according to his own expression, "bathed in sweat night and day." In winter the cold was still more unsupportable. The rain and snow entered on all sides, leaving the prisoners no refuge. And they were in most utter destitution. No one had any clothing beyond what he wore on his arrival, and of this no article was replaced, repaired, or washed. Our Saint was three years without changing his habit or shirt. The food was worthy of all the rest. "Our ordinary," wrote Blessed Charles, "consists of two dishes of boiled rice and a very disagreeable and bitter juice called Xire. To this are added some raw roots or two salt herrings." Subsequently the last articles were cut off as being too good fare. Had they been allowed a sufficient portion either of rice or roots, it would have been tolerable; but all seemed calculated down so as merely to prevent their starving to death." "One day," says another letter, "the guards brought some pieces of badly-baked bread, hard and old; we ate it as a delicious cake, so famished were we." They were starved to such a point that Gonroc grew alarmed. Fearing that they would die, he sent one Gasuémon, an inspector, to examine the circumstances and take suitable measures. The inspector agreed for some relief with the contractor for food, but that avaricious pagan found means to elude the agreement.[1] Sometimes Christians from Nagasaki succeeded in getting better food through to the martyrs; but this subjected the guards to great risks, and of their own accord the prisoners declined these marks of friendship.

More remains to be said of these various torments, nor have I said anything of that which all accounts characterize as most insupportable—the stench. "This torment," wrote Spinola, "makes me raise my sighs to heaven." And no wonder. There were thirty men crowded on one another, bathed in sweat or soaked with rain, with garments rotting on their bodies; and, to complete their misery, forced to satisfy the wants of nature in that very place. The prison soon resembled a sewer, and, at times, for example after a heavy rain, the infection became horrible—it stifled the strongest. Corruption and filth brought on another scourge—vermin. The holy confessors

---

[2] Defraudavit etiam portione victus, quam admetiri jubebatur. Letter to Father Ruiz. The contractor was bound to furnish each prisoner about ten cents worth a day.

were devoured by them; and they had not a vessel of any kind, even one of those that our habits of cleanliness make indispensable. But enough; it is more than we could credit, were not these details drawn from letters dated in the fearful dungeon of Omura.

In face of these incontestible facts the reader may ask how the victims of such barbarity could have prolonged their life for weeks, and some for several years; vigor and courage seem to afford no satisfactory explanation. We must see in it the finger of God. In some cases, in particular, God's intervention is beyond doubt; and we have an example in Father Spinola. "Two months' fever," he wrote to the General of the Society, "had reduced me to extremity; all expected to see me breathe my last, and I was ravished with joy, when, on the 4th of November, by the intercession of St. Charles (his patron), without any medical aid, I recovered my health." The Almighty doubtless reserved this noble victim; he had set him aside to be offered to him on the solemn day before the eyes of thousands of spectators. Hitherto he had merely purified him by constant illness. If God's action is less miraculous towards other prisoners, we must at least acknowledge in it the special Providence that ever watched over the elect. Two sank under the barbarous treatment: Blessed John of St. Dominic, of the order of Friars Preachers, and our saint's companion, Brother Ambrose Fernandez, who perished with cold after thirteen months' imprisonment. Most of the others fell into more or less severe diseases, and thus aggravated the miseries of themselves and their fellow prisoners. This circumstance was seldom taken into account by their jailers. They refused Spinola a glass of water to cool his burning fever, and the night that Brother Fernandez died they would not allow his companions to have a light to pay him the last rites. Tyrants and executioners combined to torture without causing death.

III.—Behavior of the Holy Prisoner.

It is consoling to contrast the heroism of charity with the ingenuities displayed in inventing torture. This we have already discerned; we could not describe the atrocities of the persecutor, without portraying the noble deportment of his victims; but it is our present purpose to study more closely the sentiments with which they were animated. Though speaking only of Blessed Father Spinola, we shall do homage to the virtues of his companions; for, notwithstanding a certain susceptibility, which, though it grieved, did not discourage, he exerted over them an indisputable influence—he inspired them with his own energy, and stimulated their courage; in a word, he was the worthy leader of that heroic band. We know not what he had to suffer, and yet, in no one of the many letters which he wrote during his imprisonment, does he fail to manifest his complete resignation to the will of God; nay, the joy he felt in undergoing the most fearful trials, and his eager desire to see his sufferings increased. After all such expressions, the thought of martyrdom regularly occurs, but accompanied with sentiments of his own unworthiness, and his acceptance of whatever God should send him.

These dispositions are of great importance in the ways of God; and the holy man speaks on the point with a great animation. His ordinary correspondent, Father Porro, having written that he would have been glad to be his companion in prison, he answers: "You are mistaken; you have too high an opinion of me. I am only a wretched sinner. It is not for want of graces; God gives me a great abundance of them; but it is because I do not profit by them as I should, and because I misuse the time which He gives me to prepare for death. I know nothing good in me except a great desire of suffering for God's sake, and an entire conformity to His will. True, I would wish to die a martyr; but I am ready to be driven from Japan or to languish a hundred years in this dungeon. My chief anxiety is to see the long duration of a life in which I offend God. I long for death that I may cease to sin; and I hope, through your prayers and those of our other fathers, to die at the stake or on the cross."

In another letter to the same Father, after having spoken of the wretched state of his health, he adds: "In a word, I feel that I am becoming exhausted, and that my end is drawing nigh. I am willing to die, and, in all my life, I never experienced more joy. Be kind enough to recommend me to God, and pardon my faults."

His actions corresponded with these words. On all occasions, whilst suffering the most cruel mortifications, he possessed his soul in unalterable patience. This sentiment generally displayed itself in a sweet serenity and admirable gaiety. In a letter to Father de Ursis, at Macao, dated December 5th, 1619, he says: "I am now terminating my first year's noviceship in Omura; and in the hope of attaining the profession which God promises in heaven, I am ready to accept many other years of probation. After all, what I have suffered is but little; I desire to suffer much more."

Virtue so exalted becomes contagious; it possesses a heavenly charm that attracts and wins hearts. Four Japanese prisoners experienced these happy effects. Being filled with respect and admiration at the sight of such heroism, they asked, as a great favor, to be admitted into the Society of Jesus. Their example was followed some time after by three others. They made their noviceship in prison under the direction of Father Spinola, and followed their master to martydom, where we shall again find them. Even the infidels themselves yielded at times to this influence; and several of the guards who had come with hostile dispositions, went away Christians. It happened one day, however, that the example and even the exhortations of the Saint encountered obstinate resistance; and, sad to say, this resistance came from two Christians, and what is even more, from two religious (not priests, however,) who were imprisoned for the faith of Christ! The fact is very remarkable.

They were two Japanese of that proud and generous character which is distinctive of their nation, sincerely attached to their religion, but mingling with their devotedness a certain amount of self-sufficiency and pride; on the least difference of opinion, they offended their companions in captivity, and took offence on the slightest occasion. This disposition manifested itself on a certain occasion, when they became irritated and obstinate. Father Spinola had, properly speaking, no authority excepting over the members of his own Order: he had thought it prudent therefore, up to this, to show his disapprobation by his silence; but, all at once, standing up like one inspired, he addressed to these two refractory individuals an energetic exhortation on concord and humility. He reminded them, in a touching manner, of the proofs they had already given of their love for God; he tenderly urged them to conform their conduct to that of their divine Model who was meek and humble of heart. All his efforts were ineffectual. Then the minister of Jesus Christ, listening only to his zeal for the glory of his Master, threatened them with the wrath of God and exemplary chastisement. They were not punished immediately: they persevered with the other confessors up to the very day of execution. When leaving the prison, the holy man declared, with tears in his eyes, *that, as formerly at Sebaste, all could not receive the crown from the hands of angels. I greatly fear*, said he frequently, *lest some among us dim the splendor of this great day by a shameful fall.* His prediction, alas! was but too truly accomplished.

Return we now to the faithful and fervent band preparing for the final combat. On such occasions, even the strongest man is no more than a weak reed, and the most lively fervor a fire that must soon die out unless it receive fuel from without. If such is the condition of Christian virtue in general, what care, what assistance must be required to keep alive in souls heroic devotedness and untiring patience! God granted that assistance to his persecuted servants; that care his servants took, and all that we have admired in them, finds an easy explanation in their co-operation with the grace of God. *Gratia Dei mecum.*

There is one grace on which, indeed, they could not have reckoned—the very fountain of all graces—the most Holy Eucharist. Still, except during the first months of captivity, they had the consolation of saying or hearing Mass every day; and never was anything essential for the Holy Sacrifice wanting, whether it was hosts, or wine, or candles. These things were furnished them by the Christians of Nagasaki; being secretly introduced, some time, by the assistance of the guards who had been converted, at other times through the connivance of the pagans. With what solicitude they watched over everything connected with the divine mysteries! With what happiness they participated in them! Father Spinola celebrated Mass every day that his health allowed it; and in his eyes, *the presence of Jesus changed their horrible dungeon into a paradise*, as he wrote to Father Sebastian Vieira, on the 20th of February, 1620. In a letter to the Rev. Father General, he develops his thought more at length: "The divine Sacrifice constitutes our sole consolation; and by a signal favor of divine Providence, we have all that is required for the service of the altar. The Bread of Life sustains both body and soul; the heavenly wine raises us above all our troubles, and makes us desirous of sacrificing our lives a thousand times for Him who, with so great love, gave Himself up for our sake."

With the daily celebration of Mass, their prison life assumed another aspect; their day had an object, a plan of life was outlined; to avoid tedium and the dangers occasioned by idleness, all that was now required was to regulate in like manner their other occupations. Father Spinola had no difficulty in causing his views on this important head to be adopted, and it is through one of his letters to the Rev. Father General, that we have been made acquainted with these particulars. One would be inclined to believe that he was reading the regulations of a convent.

First of all, a superior was elected each week, to maintain order. The day was begun with meditation during one hour, then the priests said Mass. After the Masses, the little Hours of the Canonical Office were recited, and then the Rosary. The reading of some good book followed till dinner. After this meal, they conversed on some edifying subject.

This was followed by Vespers, and still other prayers and pious readings. Before supper they said Matins for the next day and the little Office of the Blessed Virgin. On holidays the Litany of the Blessed Virgin and the hymn *Ave Maria Stella* were added. In the evening they gave a quarter of an hour to examination of conscience, which was followed, except on festivals, by a severe discipline.[1]

Some of our readers will wonder at this last exercise; did they not suffer enough otherwise without self-inflicted penances? Yet such is the last effect of the love of God in souls: an unquenchable desire to resemble Jesus crucified. The more they suffer the more they wish to suffer. "*More, O Lord, still more!*" exclaimed the first apostle of Japan; and his worthy imitator, Blessed Father Spinola, was not satisfied with the tortures he endured in prison, nor with ordinary penances laid down in the regulations. He almost continually wore a hair shirt; and even, on the small amount of food allowed the prisoners, he found means of mortifying himself. "My meals"—thus he writes to Father Pereira, then procurator of the province of Japan—"consist of two plates of rice each day, one in the morning and one in the evening." Often even he took nothing at all in the evening. If it happened that, during his illnesses, the Procurator, or any one else, sent him some little delicacy, he di-

---

[1] "Flagellationem in dies nisi festi sunt adhibemus."—Letter to Very Rev. F. Mutius Vitelleschi, Feb. 18, 1620. In another letter he says: "Peracta cum parcissimo cibo quadragesima, adhibitaque in dies singulos bene longa corporum flagellatione."

vided it all among his companions; and if, owing to the vigilance of the guards, nothing of this kind reached him, he experienced genuine satisfaction. We read the following in one of his letters to Father Porro:

"For some days past we receive no more delicacies; we are once more brought back to boiled rice. With our former diet, we have recovered all our gayety. In fact, so many presents have been thus far sent us, that we no longer resembled men imprisoned for Christ's sake, and I was afflicted. Praised be God, that he deigns to try us! I shall do my best till the hour comes fixed for me in His eternal decrees."

With respect to this eagerly desired hour, Father Spinola collected with the liveliest interest all rumors from abroad. If exile were spoken of, he was visibly grieved, and begged his friends to obtain for him the pardon of his sins, which, said he, rendered him unworthy of martyrdom. On the other hand, if the cross or the stake were spoken of, he could no longer repress his joy; he said mass for those who brought the welcome tidings. His letters about this time are full of this lofty sentiment, and his language possesses all the unction of sanctity. This it is that induces me to quote certain passages:

"At last,' writes he to a Father in Japan, "my hour is come; I clearly know the will of God in my regard; I shall leave this prison—such is my firm belief—only to go to heaven. This fills me with consolation. O Father, how liberally God has rewarded my labors by the single grace he has granted me of being imprisoned for His love! How sweet, how delicious it is to suffer for Jesus Christ! I never experienced this so vividly as since I am in this prison."

As early as the 18th of February, 1620, more than two years before his martyrdom, Blessed Spinola thus wrote to the very Rev. Father Mutius Vitelleschi, the General of the Society:

"We are subjected to the same harsh treatment, and we endeavor to support the tedium of the days and nights by exercises of piety. (*Here follow certain details already mentioned*). . . . When the news was brought to us lately, from Nagasaki, that we were to be burnt alive, as those had been who gave us hospitality, all the prisoners felt their joy and fervor redoubled. Who can tell what will be consequences of the death of the prince of Omura, who has just been cut off suddenly? His successor may cut our heads off to be rid of us. At the present time when I write to you, very reverend Father, the persecution rages against the Christians of Nagasaki, and I am persuaded that we shall feel its effects. In any case, my strength is so exhausted, that in all probability I shall be unable to write to you again. Farewell, then, very reverend Father, till we meet in heaven! I beg you, in all humility, not to forget, at the altar, this poor prisoner for Christ's sake, and to recommend him to all our Fathers and brothers. I in turn pray every day at the holy sacrifice for them all, and particularly for your paternity."

Under such circumstances, he could not forget his faithful correspondent, Father Porro. He gives that

Father the tidings of his approaching death in the following terms :

"For some days past the rumor is that we shall be burned alive in the course of this year. By the time you receive this letter, I shall, perhaps, have quitted this exile; as far as I am concerned, I long to end it at once, that I may cease offending Him, to whom I owe so much. Farewell, dear Father! we shall see each other again on the Holy Mountain, in the bosom of God!"

One year before his death, he thus writes to the same Father:

"We have it from good authority that Gonroc said in August, that we were to be burnt alive in the course of the month of September. You can easily conceive, Rev. Father, that this news has transported us with joy! Nevertheless, since then, we have received other intelligence that raises some doubt. What is beyond doubt is, that while awaiting the fire of the persecutors, it has pleased God to send three of us the fire of fever, and I have had my share. But at the same time I have received such intense spiritual consolation, that my pains were lulled in my colloquies with the Divine Majesty."

About the same time he thus opened his heart to Father Baeza,[1] rector of the college of Nagasaki:

"The good news you gave me, is a subject of un-

---

[1] This Father remained concealed at Nagasaki, with Father de Couros, the provincial, and nine of the Jesuits, till 1620. Then the two former, constantly pursued, left the city, at noon, in an open palanquin, without being recognized or even suspected by any one.

speakable joy, but I have still more positive information by a more trustworthy man, who says he heard it from Gonroc himself, that we are all to be burned alive next October. God grant it be so. O my dear Father, to be bound to a stake and burned for the love of Christ—what happiness, and this happiness to be mine! Too well I know myself unworthy of such a favor; but I know, too, that God's mercy is infinite. If what I state is not a false rumor, I embrace you with all my heart, in token of farewell, till we see each other again in heaven."

I cannot better conclude this sketch of the heroic dispositions of our Saint than by the beautiful letter which he wrote to his cousin, Maximilian Spinola. It is a summary of his whole prison life:

"These past years I have written several letters to our uncles; having received no reply I have thought that it would be sufficient henceforward to send my relatives tidings of me through the Provincial at Milan, or the rector of the college at Genoa. But Father Peter Morigione who has gone hence to Rome, and Father Nicholas Spinola having informed me that you are now, by the decease of Count Augustine, Count of Tassarolo, and that no other survives except Ferdinand, whose letter reached here last year, I can not refrain from acquainting you fully with the singular favor bestowed on me by God, of which, perhaps, some rumor has already reached you, namely, that I am in prison for preaching the faith.

"I was carried off at midnight ushering in the 14th

of December, 1618. Till the latter part of July, 1619, I was confined with my companions in a thatched cottage, not extremely inconvenient, surrounded by palisades and guards; then they drove us into this more confined prison, twenty-four palms long by sixteen wide, just recently built, like a birdcage, of thick square posts, open to the wind and rain, but safe under God's protection.

"Eight religious are now detained here: four of the order of St. Dominic, one, Father Angelo Orsucci, a native of Lucca; three of the order of Friars Minor; I am the only one of the Society of Jesus,[1] since the death of Brother Ambrose Fernandez, a Portuguese, who was captured with me and perished of cold and misery on the 7th of January last year. There are, besides, fifteen Japanese catechists or domestics.

"I have suffered much from the cramped space and want of food. Twice have I been seriously ill, and I often thought I should die of exhaustion, but God has preserved my life to enable me to suffer more for his service. At first it was said that we were to be banished to China or the Philippines; but since this new prison was erected, our persecutors say that we are to be killed by the effects of long imprisonment; that they did not wish to put us

---

[1] Soon after this letter was written (Feb. 28, 1621) the number of Jesuits was increased by the arrival of Father Kimura, a Japanese, and by the admission of the four novices mentioned already, as well as by the arrival of eight religious, three of whom belonged to his Society.

to death, as they saw us eagerly desire to witness our faith in our blood. Nor do they see that they thus torture us by a longer though more illustrious death. Who knows but that the emperor seeing that, instead of wasting away, we are alive and happy, and that this prison of ours inflames all Japan, as with a thousand sermons, will order us to execution?

"Meanwhile, by night and day, we confirm our souls by exercises of piety, we chastise our bodies by scourging, haircloths, and other like mortifications; and what constitutes our greatest consolation, we minister at the altar daily. And it has surely been by a special providence of God, that vestments and other requisites for the holy sacrifices were introduced unseen by the guards, after we had been at first for several months deprived of them and unable to refresh ourselves with the heavenly bread of angels.

"For my own part I am overjoyed at this special benefit of God, accomplishing the desire which chiefly brought me hither, and I esteem it above the splendor of all fleeting dignities. And justly, for St. Paul, after being once imprisoned triumphed more in the glory of his chains and bonds, than in his very apostleship, calling himself 'Bound in the Lord.' I blush for shame when I think how by no merit of mine I have obtained this great grace; how God, having before him so many holy persons, who have cultivated this vineyard with such admirable zeal, has cast his eyes on me, the last of all in the gifts of nature and merit. Again, however, the words of St.

Paul console me: "Not of the willer, nor of the runner, but of God that showeth mercy." Rom. ix. 16.

"And, indeed, we frequently see this grace denied by the divine Majesty to men renowned for exalted sanctity, who sought it with earnest prayers, and granted to men steeped in sin, to show that it was to be obtained only by divine favor and not granted to our good works.

"I have been desirous of writing this to you, and through you to the rest of my kindred, that you may rejoice to have a kinsman captive for Christ and doomed to death. The cause of my imprisonment is my unwillingness to leave Japan, when the king ordered all religious to depart, my superiors having consented to my remaining, that I might watch over the Christians, gain new converts, by the help of other Fathers of our own and other orders. Let them thank God for this, and have masses said for me, and obtain from me the glory of this distinction, that I go not forth alive from this dungeon, unless to the cross or the stake. Let them justly esteem this glory more than any rank, dignity or fortune they enjoy, as these, unless adorned by an upright life and the observance of God's law, or freely bestowed in charity on the poor or religious, are obstacles to eternal salvation. Let them think of the instability of this life and the certainty of death, which strips them unawares of all this world's goods, leaving them nothing but their virtues to bear with them. Let them understand fully the value of toil and suffering endured for God. By this thought and the divine grace, many with unshaken magnanimity have despised rank, wealth, dignities, liberty and kingdoms, even the empire itself, to retire to the desert or to cloisters, to pass their lives in the exercises of penance, meditating on the life and death of our Saviour, conforming their lives to his perpetual humility and want!

"O my kinsmen! could you but taste the delights which the most benignant Jesus imparts to those who serve him or endure sufferings for his sake, you would see clearly how hollow are the pleasures which this world promises but cannot give ; as they cannot satisfy the vastness of that soul created for God alone.

"I, who can aver that I now begin to be a disciple of Christ amid the greatest pain and confinement of prison, even when my strength seemed failing from hunger alone, I was always refreshed by such delights of consolation, that I deemed all my sufferings undergone in the divine service richly rewarded. Were I still to pass several years in this dungeon, the time would seem to me short in my intense desire of suffering for His love, who so lavishly rewards the labors of this life and makes even torture itself sweet and desirable. Yet God is to be served chiefly for himself alone, for He is the fountain of all goodness, and merits all our devotion without any hope of reward.

"Among the various diseases by which my health has been tried in prison, a continual and dangerous fever seized and afflicted me for a hundred days.

Destitute of all human remedies, with no food suited to a sick person, I despaired of my recovery, as did all my companions. Then my heart was too full of joy, for such joy I never remember to have felt, so that I bounded in exultation and seemed at the very threshold of heaven. If God thus consoles the sufferings of his servants here on earth, what must be the delights which he has prepared in heaven, the real place of reward?

"Let us then serve so good, so clement a God, nor deem it difficult to moderate the fierce impulses of passion or chastise our body, in the assurance that if we suffer here with Christ we shall reign with him eternally in heaven, which no man reaches but by suffering.

"I commend me especially to Ferdinand and Alexander Spinola, and the daughters of the late Fabricius Spinola and my other kinsfolk. I bid a last farewell to them and my native land, for I feel so enfeebled that I doubt whether I shall survive to the next occasion of writing. I remember you all daily at the altar; nor shall I forget you if God finds me worthy to enter his heavenly Jerusalem. Farewell, farewell, till we meet again in heaven.

"From my prison at Omura, February 28th, 1621.

"CHARLES,

"Imprisoned for the Faith of Christ."

IV.—REMOVAL TO FIRANDO.

We have followed Blessed Spinola through that long series of fearful trials down to the moment when everything foretokened a bloody close. Before describing the last act of the heroic drama, we must retrace events somewhat.

In consequence of the dissensions between the Portuguese and the Dutch, piracy spread in the East, and scourged especially the Japan seas. In 1621, some English and Dutch pirates seized a Japanese vessel off the island of Formosa, while on its way from the Philippines to Nagasaki. Among the passengers were two Spaniards whose exterior had nothing uncommon, but whom the pirates from some mark, or from conjecture, took to be religious in disguise. This was precisely what they needed to cover the illegality of their conduct. They entered the port of Firando, and handed over to the authorities the two Spaniards together with Joachim Firaiama, the captain of the captured vessel. They pretended that they seized the vessel, not for plunder, but out of respect for the emperor's edicts, which those religious had ventured to infringe. Had the governor of Nagasaki consulted only his hatred against the Christians, he would not have failed to welcome these charges, but the question had another aspect to him. The vessel, when taken, was steering to the port confided to him; if proved that the two passengers were religious, he might be accused himself of connivance, or at least of negligence in discharging his duty. Several missionaries had already slipped in by stealth; all these clandestine movements might be laid to his charge, and then what could he expect from the emperor? He accordingly declared that the two passengers were not religious; and he boldly wrote to that purport to the emperor. The Dutch, however, to clear themselves of piracy, maintained the contrary, and affecting great friendship for the Japanese, constantly affirmed that the two men were Spaniards, religious and priests, who, under the pretext of extending their religion, came to inspect the country. This old calumny always produced a great impression.

The two religious—for such they really were—had, from the first, avowed that they were Christians, but no more. They desired with all their heart to declare themselves also priests and religious, to receive the palm of martyrdoms, but did charity permit them? Their avowal would expose the captain, who had received them aboard, to capital punishment; the rigor of the edicts on this point left no doubt. They must then find means of making themselves known, without compromising Captain Joachim.

While they were thus consulting, the Dutch and English were not idle. There was, they averred, very easy means of ascertaining the truth; this was to bring some religious from the Omura prison and confront them with the suspected individuals. This was done, and we possess a circumstantial report from Blessed Charles to the Provincial of Japan.

One evening in November, after supper time, they led out of prison Father Francis Morales, a Dominican, Father Peter de Avila, a Franciscan, and Father Charles Spinola. At the barrack they were told that they were going to start for Firando, about ninety miles distant. They respectfully asked for clothes or coverings to protect them from the cold, in consequence of the severity of the season; they were not heard, but driven aboard almost without clothes. The boat was small, and the only cabin was occupied by the two officers of the prince who commanded the guards. The Fathers, closely confined, had a small unsheltered corner, so narrow that they could scarcely move. The first night was spent in a fort overlooking the sea. The next night they reached Firando. The prisoners were placed in a cabin, near the governor's, under double guards.

On the 25th of November, after noon, the three Fathers were taken to the castle through curious crowds who flocked to the sight. Their aspect was indeed most strange. They wore the long habit of their profession, but worn to rags; their beard and hair long and neglected; attenuated, pale, unrecognizable, living skeletons, loaded with chains, they excited the compassion of the most indifferent. The Christians in the crowd saluted them as they passed, showing as well as they could their veneration and sorrow. In the plain that stretched before the castle some Portuguese awaited them, and one of them, Louis de Figueredo, fell at their feet and respectfully kissed their chains.

On entering the palace, the prisoners, after a few moments delay in the vestibule, were led into the governor's room. With him were the prince of Firando, Gonroc, governor of Nagasaki, as well as the two renegades, Feizo and Xacuemon. Among those present were some Portuguese and the English pirates. The three religious were introduced before them all, and the Blessed Spinola was asked, "Do you know these Spaniards?" "No," he replied, "I have not been out of Japan for twenty years; I never saw them." The two other religious made similar replies.

This confronting led to no result. Feizo then addressed Blessed Charles this captious question: "Is a religious or priest permitted to deny that he is such?" The apostate knew that a Christian was bound to confess himself a Christian in presence of a judge, and thinking it the same with the sacerdotal character, he wished to condemn the two disguised religious by one of their brethren; but Blessed Charles explained the difference, and replied that, in certain cases, the priest or religious was not obliged to reveal his character. Then an Englishman boldly said: "That is true; so they do in England; the priests deny it, to avoid punishment." "You are mistaken," replied Blessed Spinola, "and I prove it by my own example. I, too, was taken by an English pirate, and although I knew your animosity against me, and the cruelty of your tortures, I declared distinctly that I was a priest and a religious of the Society of Jesus. I know, too, that several other Jesuits have done the same, and shed their blood for the faith. You know yourself, my lord, by your own experience," said he, turning to Gonroc, "how we act on this point, and this testimony is better than that of an Englishman." These words silenced him and closed the examination.

Before he withdrew, the ardent apostle endeavored to recall the wretched Feizo to the way of salvation; he approached him and begged him to grant him a short interview. The apostate, divining his intention, declined, alleging the frivolous excuse that he had no time. Our Saint could then only remind him briefly of his former protestations, the graces he had received, and the chastisements to which he exposed himself, as the implacable persecutor of those whom he had loved as his brethren. The apostate could not bear these apostolic words: he grew pale, and without saying a word he withdrew covered with shame, to appear no more.

Louis Figueredo did not neglect the confessors of the faith: he asked Gonroc permission to receive them at his table, to send them clothing and other necessary articles in the prison of Omura. Gonroc himself could not witness such miseries united to such merit without a sentiment of compassion, and he granted the request. The other Portuguese, having been informed of this condescension, considered it an honor to contribute largely to the good work, in favor of the thirty-two captives in the prison of Omura. But their charity was a reproach to the apostate Feizo; he counted the garments offered, and admitted but a small number of them. Figueredo in vain supplicated on his knees; the barbarian was inexorable. A terrible example of the hardness of heart to which he falls a victim, who has been guilty of perjury to his God, and become a traitor to Jesus Christ!

The principal affair remained still unsettled. The judges, having no certain proof against the two Spaniards, wished, as it was said at the palace, to administer the oath to them. But the prisoners refused, protesting against the illegality of such a proceeding. This refusal seeming to wound the delicacy of the Christians, Father Spinola became the interpreter of their sentiments. Having obtained permission to speak privately to the two religious, he represented to them that common edification should outweigh the captain's interest, and that it only remained to speak the truth. This was all they desired. They accordingly declared that they were priests and religious, the one Peter de Zuñiga, of the order of St. Augustine; the other, Louis Flores,[1] of the order of St. Dominic. In making this declaration, they took every possible precaution in favor of Captain Joachim; on his side, Blessed Charles made application to Gonroc and the Prince of Firando, but in vain. He had no greater success in his endeavors to exercise his zeal among the people: he was kept isolated and brought back with his companions to the prison of Omura. His journey had no other effect than to

---

[1] Or rather Fraryn. See the notice of this martyr in the appendix.

bring on him a catarrh, from which he suffered all winter, and the merit of immovable patience.

V.—The Condemnation.

The declaration of the two religious had thrown the ambitious Gonroc into a terrible state of embarrassment. It was a contradiction of the positive and repeated affirmations by which he had led his sovereign into error. What might he not expect from the Emperor's wrath when he learned the truth? The only chance of safety for Gonroc was to be prompt, and whilst acknowledging the facts, explain them, and, in as much as possible, allay the violence of the first outbursts. For this end, after having provided for the safe keeping of the prisoners, he repaired to the capital, obtained an audience, and related what had occurred. The emperor, at the recital, became violently angry: "What audacity!" he cried; "these men already banished and proscribed, dare to set my edicts at defiance, and enter my empire by stealth! And there are to be found Japanese to conduct them hither! What further remains for them, if it be not to seize the supreme power?"

At this moment a courier arrives from Firando, to announce to the emperor that one of the two religious had attempted to escape from prison, and had well nigh succeeded. In fact, Father Flores, detained on a rock not far from Firando, had succeeded with the aid of some neophytes in embarking, but he was overtaken, bound, and brought back to prison. This exasperated Xongun beyond all bounds. He said to Gonroc, " This is all your fault; had I given to another the charge I confided to you, Japan would now be delivered from all these foreign Bonzes, who come to disturb my empire by preaching a law contrary to all our sects. It is because you do not keep a strict enough watch over the vessels that enter your ports, that these priests daily arrive. Return promptly to Nagasaki and burn alive those two religious who lately arrived there, with the captain who brought them. Put to the same torture all the priests and religious whom you will find, whether Europeans or Japanese. Spare neither their hosts, nor the wives of their hosts, their children of what age soever they may be, nor even the Christians who inhabit the neighboring houses; off with all their heads; and treat in like manner all the crew of the captured vessel. I wish, moreover, that the wives and children of those who have been put to death within the last three years for the Christian religion, or who are still in prison for the same cause, be likewise put to death. Make every effort to discover the religious who are still secreted in Japan, and take care that not one enter henceforth : for, if through your fault, trouble arise in the State, your head must pay the penalty."

Such was the sentence of the emperor Xongun, who inaugurated the great era of the martyrs of Japan; in a few days one hundred and twenty persons were put to death for their religion, and during ten years Christian blood ceased not to bedew an ungrateful soil. Gonroc returned to Nagasaki, stunned by the menaces of his master. Of himself, he was not cruel; we have seen him accessible to compassion; but as the tool of a tyrant, he was capable of proceeding to any excess. Besides, self-interest stimulated him on this occasion; he had to regain the favor of Xongun, and he immediately strove to give him proofs of his devotedness. He commenced by causing the arrest of all included in the sentence of the emperor, and he increased the guard and redoubled all the precautions against the prisoners. On the 19th of August, 1622, he caused the two religious and the captain to be burned alive, and beheaded twelve Christian sailors who all suffered death with an admirable constancy.

When intelligence of this execution reached Omura, and the edict of the emperor was there made known, the joy of the holy confessors was inexpressible. We know with what sentiments they awaited the blessed hour of their sacrifice, and behold it is near! They can no longer doubt it. They hold themselves in readiness, and bid farewell from a distance to their relatives and friends. The letters which they wrote on that occasion, and which fortunately escaped the vigilance of the guards, recalled the letters of Cyprian and of Ignatius[1] of the primi-

---

[1] The "Revue Catholique" for May, 1867, contains the beautiful letter of Blessed Richard of St. Anne, a Belgian religious of the order of St. Francis, to his colleagues of Nivelles.

tive church. Blessed Charles Spinola wrote to his superiors and to some other Fathers, and left his last advice to the members of the Sodality of Nagasaki. We extract from his letters what appears of greatest interest:

"To the Reverend Father Provincial:

"Yesterday our prison was visited by our guards in a sort of fury. We thought they came to massacre or lead us to Nagasaki, but it was to take the names of the prisoners. We have learned of the beautiful death of those who had arrived from Manilla. I hope that we, like them, shall soon be burned. We are, with the grace of God, ready for everything, and in expectation of the happy moment. Ineffable goodness and mercy of God! that a wretch like myself shall have the happiness and glory to die for love of Him! May I also, through your prayers, through the intercession of Mary and the saints, be sufficiently strong in body and soul to sustain this last combat as becomes a child of the Society of Jesus! Besides, it appears to me that God has prepared us for this for a year, and above all, during the last two months, with the attention of a master of novices. He permitted the guards to be more severe, and the food worse. We no longer have the consolation of receiving letters. Nevertheless the greatest of all consolations has not been wanting; by a special protection of Heaven we have always hosts and wine for the Holy Sacrifice.

"In bidding you farewell, reverend Father, I feel a

desire to cast myself at your feet and ask pardon for all my faults, particularly for having profited so little by the means of sanctification which were offered me during these four years imprisonment. . . . I beg all my Fathers and Brothers, whom I embrace for the last time with all my heart, to help to thank God for me, and to obtain for me constancy in the decisive trial. I enclose in this letter two reliquaries containing precious mementoes : one is a piece of the sack which Saint Ignatius wore after his conversion, and which has wrought many miracles; the other containing a relic of the Blessed Aloysius Gonzaga, sent to me by our reverend Father General. I have added some of Brother Ambrose Fernandez' hair. I also send you the pictures which I had placed in my breviary; if you will have the kindness to distribute them, they will recall me to the remembrance of our Fathers in Japan and Macao who knew me. If God grants me the grace of admitting me to the holy mountain, I shall never forget either you or our dear Province.

"CHARLES,
"Condemned to death for the
"Name of Jesus."
AUGUST 28, 1622.

The letter to Father Baeza, rector of Nagasaki, contains similar details; but we read, in that which is addressed to Father Jerome Ruiz, visitor of China and of Japan, the following lines :

"In consequence of the new severities of which we were the object, I have had to struggle against hunger and weakness. Father Sebastian (Kimura) and my novices suffered like myself, and some of my companions (we were thirty-two) appeared ready to expire. Now I am only skin and bone, and until to-day I have not been able to stand without feeling dizzy. Praised be God, who appears to wish to preserve all to be offered to Him as holocausts:

"Sarabà, sarabà (a Japanese word, meaning adieu).
August 30, 1622.
"CHARLES,
"Condemned to death for the
"Christian Faith."

The executions which had previously taken place, whether at Nagasaki or in the other parts of the empire, were only the prelude to what has been justly styled "The Great Martyrdom." Gonroc became more furious as time went on; the smell of blood seemed to intoxicate him. At Omura, he had select victims: he caused them to be counted, and "in a few days," said he to the governor Ficoiemon, "I will rid you of all these!"

Ficoiemon was accordingly ordered to convey to Omura all the prisoners arrested within the limits of the government of Nagasaki. He repaired to the prison with a body of soldiers, and sent in four guards, who seized the confessors one by one, bound their hands and delivered them to the escort. There were twenty-four religious; the other prisoners, namely, two religious and six Japanese, not having been arrested within the territory of Nagasaki, were reserved to undergo, on the third day, the same fate at Omura.

This separation occasioned a very touching scene, in which the noblest sentiments were manifested on both sides. Charles and his companions were radiant with happiness; already they beheld heaven open to receive them; the others saw, with a holy envy, the departure of those with whom they expected to triumph as they had suffered together. They mingled their tears in a last embrace; they sang together the canticle of their deliverance. It was on the 9th of September, Friday, a day consecrated by the captives to penance in honor of the passion of our Lord: the future martyrs drew new strength from this thought, rejoicing to sanctify, by fasting, the eve of their triumph.

They set out. At the foot of the hill of Suzuta, a large junk was prepared for the prisoners, and several small craft for their escort. The latter had received orders to let no one approach under any pretext, and even to prevent all communication; but it was scarcely possible to restrain the zeal of the confessors of the Faith. During the few hours' passage across the bay of Omura, they constantly exhorted the soldiers, the sailors, and all within the reach of their voices, to remain faithful if they were Christians—to become Christians if they were not such already, and to do penance if they had had the misfortune to yield to torments. "It is for you," said they, "for your eternal happiness that we came, and we now bear with joy fire and the sword."

Having reached Naga or Nagaia,[1] some miles from

---
[1] Others say the fort Nangaia. This must be a mistake: the fort

Nagasaki, they were obliged to mount on horseback in order to escape the importunity of the Christians of that locality. The procession was thus arranged: a superior officer rode first, accompanied by a large number of guards armed with lances and muskets; the confessors, Spinola at their head, amid a company of soldiers, followed, one after another, a rope around their necks, each one having an executioner, who held the end of the rope. Then came three officers, and finally, to close the procession, a guard, which, with those on the flanks, made the escort amount to three or four hundred men. Besides their customary arms, these guards had large bamboo canes to keep the Christians at a distance. After marching six miles in this order, they halted for the night at Uracam, a place in the territory of Nagasaki. It was another night of suffering for the confessors.

Although their end was so near, they were all ignorant of the kind of torture to which they were destined. Father Spinola was informed of it only at break of day and after this manner. Three Christians, one of them Blessed Spinola's catechist, succeeded in gaining access to the prisoners. This catechist came to ask the last blessing of Blessed Charles; and he obtained more than he hoped. The holy man also gave him the discipline he had made use of during his imprisonment. On his side, as if to show the price he attached to this relic, and his gratitude, the

---

of Nangaia lies to the north of Omura, in an opposite direction to that of Nagasaki.

catechist announced to his beloved Father that the stake was prepared for him. These words completed the happiness of the generous martyr! Before the close of the day his sweetest hopes should be realized!

Gonroc, in hopes of regaining the favor of his sovereign, resolved to manifest on this occasion the greatest rigor. He wished to acquire with the emperor a reputation for severity, and strike terror among the Christians, too numerous, in his opinion, to be subjected to the same chastisement. With this view there were to be assembled at the same place and hour, united in the same holocaust, the twenty-four religious of Omura, and the thirty-one Christians detained at Nagasaki; while the heads of the accomplices fell by the sword, the fire was to be slowly consuming the great culprits. No one was to converse with the condemned or pass the limits marked; but at that distance spectators were to have every liberty, and the governor would have no objection to see an immense crowd gather. From a very different motive our saint rejoiced at all this preparation; he beheld in it a triumph for faith and an exhortation to martyrdom. In order to appear worthily at this festival, he had had two surplices of pure white prepared, in advance, for himself and Father Sebastian Kimura, and new habits for the seven other Jesuits, his novices, whom he had just admitted to their vows. But even this did not suffice to exalt religion in the eyes of the idolaters. They, too, affected pomp and display when death was to be confronted, and Christian devotedness was to be clearly distinguished from pagan pride. Blessed Charles had prepared a standard, bearing, in large letters, the holy name of Jesus, surrounded by rays, the whole of precious stuff and elegantly embroidered. He proposed to carry this labarum from his entrance into Nagasaki till he stood amid the flames; but Gonroc feared the effect of such a demonstration and forbade him to carry it out. Perhaps, too, it was better that the martyrs of Christ should, like their divine model, be made a spectacle with all the externals of suffering and misery.

The day had come, and the sun was already rising above the horizon; after a slight collation, the cortege of prisoners and guards proceeded to Nagasaki in the same order and with the same precautions as on the previous day. The road was lined with spectators, and as they approached the city the crowd increased. These were especially Christians, coming bathed in tears to salute the martyrs of the faith, ask their blessing, and commend themselves to their prayers. "What," they cried, " will become of our once flourishing church when we have no longer any pastors?" Their grief was intense and their lamentations heart-rending. The confessors replied with emotion by marks of affection and especially by courageous exhortations. "Our prayers shall never fail you, if, as we hope, we are going to heaven. But do you be true to yourselves; suffer all rather than lose the faith. Be faithful till death, to the stake." These and similar words they were obliged to repeat incessantly to all the groups studding the three miles between Uracam and Nagasaki. They did not enter the city, for Gonroc foresaw that in the streets his police would be powerless to suppress an outbreak; the martyrs were led straight to the place of execution, where a scene awaited them whose imposing solemnity words cannot convey. But to understand all the details of the martyrdom, it requires some description of the spot.

The city of Nagasaki lies on the west coast of the island of Ximo, at the head of a picturesque bay that forms its harbor. On the land side it is shut in by a continuous range of mountains, except on the northeast, where the road comes in from Omura and the kingdom of Figen. This road before reaching Nagasaki skirts on the right an elevated table-land, which advances some distance into the bay. This promontory stands out so clearly to the eye from the landscape in the background, that at a distance it would be taken for an island. On the other side of the road, the ground rises gradually to a very great height. It is a natural amphitheatre, capable of holding an incalculable number of spectators, and from all the points of this immense semicircle the eye rests on the promontory plateau. This eminence had attracted the attention of all the persecutors, and been time again steeped in Christian blood. In 1597 it had witnessed the courage of twenty-six martyrs crucified for the faith and now honored by the church with public cultus, and from that day the people never designated it under any name but "The Sacred Mountain." This same place Gonroc had selected for the execution.

At the extremity of the promontory, on an eminence, rose a richly-decorated platform, covered with China carpets, and surrounded by the insignia of authority and justice. There, with his fellow-functionary, was to sit the cruel Suquendaiu, appointed by Gouroc to preside at the execution. From this dominant point, facing the mountain, he could follow the movements of the confessors almost at his feet, as well as of the more distant spectators. Two parallel lines stretched across the table land—one for the victims destined to perish by the sword; the other for those condemned to the stake. The first had only the places marked out; the second was formed of twenty-five stakes, with piles of wood around at a distance of six yards. The arena occupied by these preparations was enclosed by a paling strong enough to resist an ordinary pressure, and low enough to leave all visible that took place inside. The approaches to this enclosure were guarded by an imposing force: the lancers of Firando on the seaside—the musketeers of Omura at the foot of the mountain. These precautions would have been unavailing had the Christians had any idea of revolt; under the actual circumstances they were superfluous.

The crowd that gathered to witness the scene surpassed all that could have been anticipated. It covered the mountain and occupied all the favorable points along the bay. It was estimated that there were thirty thousand Christians besides the pagans. They were the whole population of Nagasaki and its neighborhood. Long before the appointed hour, all, especially the Christians, were there in feverish expectation; their eyes now fixed on the stakes already in their imagination lit up by the flames, then on the Omura road, where every moment they seemed to see the head of the noble procession. At last it appears. As soon as it was well in sight, and they began to recognize the countenances of the prisoners, such a clamor arose, mingled with sobs and sighs of joy, that not a word could be heard. During this time the confessors had advanced to the foot of the mountain, where they awaited the arrival of the prisoners from Nagasaki. This halt allowed the emotion to subside, and the holy victims to be better examined. All eyes were fixed on Father Spinola, so known, yet so past recognition—not only aged and disfigured, but emaciated, scarce able to stand; but with all this his countenance shone with the beauty peculiar to holiness, and his features expressed a heavenly joy which reached the heart and called forth tears of devotion.

After a delay of an hour, the prisoners from Nagasaki appeared. Besides the men, there were several women and five children, three of them very young. Most of them were condemned to lose their heads. The barbarous decree of Xongun turned into a crime the hospitality they had given to religious, or the fact of being wife or child of such a host, or simply having lived in the neighborhood. They might, indeed, have saved their heads by abjuring their religion; but when cited before Goñroc they had confessed the faith with unshaken courage. This noble band arrived singing, followed from their prison by a pious multitude, mourning especially over the fate of the children carried to execution in their mothers' arms. The meeting of the two companies of martyrs was worthy and cordial. Reciprocal congratulations, marks of esteem and affection were exchanged till the inclosure was opened and the executioners began their task.

At an order of the President, the thirty who were to be beheaded were brought in and placed on the designated line opposite the stakes. Then the twenty-five others (this number is now well settled), who were to perish by fire, were taken to their stakes, each by a special executioner appointed to bind him. The custom was, to bind the person so that he could not escape from his bonds; now, the contrary was done. Only the hands of the confessors were tied, and so slightly, that by the least effort, they would be free in all their movements; and, to facilitate flight still more, vacant spaces were left between the piles of wood.

The first stakes, beginning from the seashore, were assigned to Japanese: Anthony Sanga, Paul Nangasci, Anthony of Corea, and Lucy de Freitas the widow of a Portuguese. Father Charles Spinola was led to the fifth stake. Then followed three Dominicans—Fathers Angelo Orsucci, Joseph of St. Hyacinth, and Hyacinth Orfanel: then the Jesuit Father Sebastian Kimura, followed by six other Dominican and Franciscan friars—Fathers Richard of St. Anne, Alphonsus de Mena, Peter de Avila, Vincent of St. Joseph, Francis Morales, Leo de Satzuma. After them came five of the scholastics formed by Father Spinola—Anthony Chiuni, Gonsalvo Fusai, Thomas Acafosci, Peter Sampo, and Michael Xumpo; between this last and Louis Cavara were the wretched three who took flight. The last stake was that of the Dominican Brother, Alexis. There were three more to be burned, but as there were no more stakes they were beheaded. Among them was John Ciongocu, a disciple of Blessed Spinola. All these details are known by the depositions of eye-witnesses; there has even been preserved a Japanese painting executed by one of these witnesses, representing the confessors, each at his stake and the twenty-one religious in the habits of their several orders.

When Blessed Spinola was led to his stake, he could not contain his joy and gratitude. He fell on his knees, kissed the instrument of his martyrdom, and performed these acts with such sincere respect, that all present burst forth, as by a sympathetic movement, in a unanimous acclamation. The pious martyr rose and was tied to the stake. There was nothing to do except to draw the swords and light the fires. Then amid the silence, natural at that moment of attention and anxiety, Spinola solemnly intoned the psalm "Laudate Dominum omnes gentes" —Praise the Lord all ye nations! His companions took it up with joy, and from all sides the Christians raised to heaven those accents of gratitude. "Never," said witnesses subsequently, "never did we hear anything so sweet; it was ravishing, it was heavenly." Many were convinced that angelic voices mingled with the voices of the martyrs, and in a juridical investigation that took place at Manilla, Gonsalvo Montero de Carvalho made a formal deposition in support of this opinion. All present were certainly electrified, enthusiasm gained the most indifferent, and the very pagans were moved to tears.

Our Saint, ever attentive to the occasions God afforded his zeal, seized this moment to proclaim his apostolic words. Turning towards Suquendaiu, who was quite near him, "You see what the European religious come to seek in Japan. Their joy at the sight of this fearful torture shows you the injustice of your suspicions and your prejudices against them. The Christian religion does not lead us who had renounced all this world's goods for Christ's sake, to covet your lands and your dignities. What we seek is the salvation of your souls. We are happy to give our lives for so noble a cause. Do not imagine that by our death you will alarm the preachers of the gospel and prevent their coming to Japan; on the contrary, this will draw them. From the ashes of a single one a hundred others will rise, who, inheriting our courage, will also glorify God in their mortal bodies." Then addressing the assembled multitude he said: "This fire that is about to consume us is but the shadow of that with which the true God will punish for eternity all who refuse to acknowledge him, or who, after acknowledging Him, do not live according to the sanctity of his law." To the Portuguese whom he beheld present he then addressed so touching an exhortation, that one of the chief among them, as

Father Benedict Fernandez attests in a letter, formed the resolution to leave the world and enter the Society of Jesus.

The President, in haste, put an end to these demonstrations; he ordered the execution to begin by those to be beheaded. Among these were Elizabeth Fernandez with her little Ignatius, baptized by our Saint on the eve of his arrest and now four years old. She was a widow, for her husband, Dominic Georgi, had been burnt alive on the 15th of November, 1619, for having given hospitality to Father Spinola. It is related that on hearing of his father's death, little Ignatius exclaimed that he would be a martyr too. Then turning to his mother, he said with an assured air, "Yes, I shall be a martyr, and you, too, dear mother, but my sister will not,"—a prediction verified in every syllable by the event. The child could not see a sabre without transports of joy, in the thought of the happiness that awaited him. When he made a present to any one, he never failed to say, "Keep it, for I am going to be a martyr," and then he would relate the most wonderful dreams. His mother had had the same presentiments in her childhood, and her whole life had been but a preparation for martyrdom. She entered the arena holding a crucifix in one hand and her beads in the other, and singing the "Laudate Dominum omnes gentes." When about to receive the fatal blow she saluted Father Spinola, who then recognized her. Little Ignatius was behind his mother, and the holy man did not see him. But a sweet recollection awoke in his heart: "Where is my little Ignatius, he exclaimed, "what have you done with him?" "Here he is," replied the mother, taking him up in her arms, "I would not deprive him of the only happiness I could afford him." The child was radiant with joy, and, like all the Christians, dressed in his finest clothes. His mother said : "See, my dear son, this is Father Charles, who made you a child of God; ask his blessing." Then the innocent child knelt down, clasped his hands and asked the blessing of the holy missionary. Father Spinola, unable to lift his bound hands, raised his eyes to heaven and cast them down on the child with an indescribable expression of happiness. At this sight, a cry of admiration and pity burst from every lip ; to repress it, the signal for the execution was given. The executioners struck off two or three heads which fell at the feet of little Ignatius ; he did not seem alarmed. They came to his mother ; he saw her head fall off without betraying any terror. He himself with an intrepidity not to be explained naturally in such a tender age, bowed his head and received the death stroke. Sublime child ! thy name shall be celebrated in the most solemn acts of the Church on earth ;[1] but who shall describe the splendors and joys of thy reception in heaven !

As soon as the first company consummated their sacrifice, the thirty heads were ranged in front of those to be burned and the fire was lighted. At the

---

[1] The Brief of Beatification gives a magnificent eulogy of the Boy Martyr.

same moment from the bay, the mountains, from all sides, rose a confused murmur. It was the public prayer of the Christians for the confessors of the faith; the solemn application of the Church to obtain for them the grace of perseverance at that decisive moment. The trial was terrible indeed. Every calculation had been made to prolong the fiery torture, by managing the distance, the quantity of fuel, the direction of the smoke. As soon as the fire burned up intensely, the attendants carefully moderated it; the victims were to be literally roasted. Some, like Father Kimura, suffered thus for three hours.

In this position Father Spinola had the courage to think of his companions. The stake of Lucy de Freitas was near his as he had desired. He gave her the last absolution. Soon after, the fire having consumed the poor woman's dress, her modesty was shocked; the missionary exhorted her to bear this confusion for love of Him to whom she had offered her sufferings and death. But the great anxiety of the holy martyr was his fear lest some of his companions might yield. Should this happen what a loss! what a scandal! This anxiety, that had not ceased since they left their prison, now grew more intense. "Be not astonished," he said to the executioners, "if you perceive any weakness. We are not made of iron, our bodies are mortal, sensible to pain. Still I trust that God will give us strength to suffer courageously for his glory." It was so at first, but when the fire burned in all its devouring activity, three Japanese rushed from their stakes, leaped through the fagots, and, invoking the gods of Japan, implored the President's clemency. Either from contempt for their cowardice, or rage at the constancy of all the rest, that officer coldly ordered them to be cast back into the flames, and horrible to relate they perished apostates, when, but a moment before, they seemed to hold the martyr's palm.[1]

After this melancholy defection, the holy martyrs, to the number of twenty-two, were slowly consumed, before the eyes of the Christians who persevered in prayer. Blessed Spinola was the first to die. He was of a delicate constitution, and in consequence of his imprisonment in a state of extreme debility; yet it was an accidental cause that hastened his death. Some sparks from the fagots falling on his habit set it on fire, and the flames rapidly reached the principal organs. As soon as he saw that no duty bound him longer to earth, he collected himself, and calmly raising his eyes to heaven, offered to God the sacrifice of his life. While the fire consumed him, he stood as long as he could straight and motionless; then sud-

[1] The process of canonization has cleared up all the essential par ticulars as to these unhappy men. There is only an unimportant doubt as to the culpability of the third apostate. According to some witnesses he did not formally apostatize, or at all events retracted. But he is not numbered among the martyrs any more than the other two. It is well here to correct an important error in Bartoli's History of Japan, where Paul Nangasci is named as one of the three. This noble martyr was in a different part of the line, and when the wretched men passed his stake he called to them earnestly, endeavoring to detain them. In this way only was he connected with them.

denly sank down, and prostrate, as if in a last prayer, gave up his soul to God, and went to heaven to receive the palm he had so well merited. He was fifty-eight years of age.

For three days the bodies of the fifteen martyrs were guarded on the scene of the execution, and, except the head of Mary Tocuan, who was a relative of the governor, they were all burned with their stakes and everything belonging to them. The ashes were collected in bags and cast into the sea. Even the bloodstained earth was removed. This was the first time that such precautions had been taken against the veneration of the faithful. But what can men effect against saints whom God chooses to glorify. Before the very eyes of the guards an extraordinary light for several nights illumined the sacred mountain—as testified by witnesses—the brilliancy was visible out at sea, as if a reflection of the immortal light enjoyed by the souls of the martyrs in heaven—as a forerunner of the glory with which Jesus will one day crown them in the day of his triumph.

PART V.

BEATIFICATION.

I.—Examination of the Case.

It belongs to the supreme authority of the church of Christ to regulate public worship, and propose to the veneration of the faithful those of her children who enjoy the Beatific vision. Before decreeing such honors, it subjects to a most rigorous examination the acts and virtues, the life and death of the person, and does not pronounce but with a full knowledge of the case, and after having long implored the light of the Holy Ghost. The rigor of the proceedings varies however according to the nature of the case. In the case of one who terminated his career by a natural death, the life must have been sanctified by heroic virtues, and his presence in heaven attested by indisputable miracles. In the case of those who have suffered death for Christ, it is less severe, or rather, it is so in a different manner. As martyrdom has, like a second baptism, the power to efface all past faults and all debts contracted towards divine justice, examination of the previous life of the martyr would be superfluous—that of miracles even is not indispensable. This last point has been doctrinally treated anew in the process of the Japanese martyrs, and decided as just stated. But, on the other hand, the martyrdom itself is subjected to the most minute investigations. The material fact of death endured for the faith and in that act of violence, the real motive of the persecutor, on the one hand—and on the other, the disposition of the victim, are the special object of the process.

Every process of this kind is introduced by the notoriety of the facts, then by official reports, and finally by the solicitations of the faithful, and especially of constituted bodies. Some details of the proceedings observed on these occasions, will not be out of place here.

The fact of the great martyrdom was witnessed by a multitude of witnesses; it soon had an immense notoriety, and excited the whole Catholic world. As soon as the sacred congregation of Rites at Rome received official accounts of this, it urged the apostolic Nuncio at Madrid and the Bishop of Macao to institute a formal inquiry. This inquest took place without delay, and produced, in 1625, thirty-two authentic depositions. In 1626, Father Sebastian Vieira, procurator of the Jesuit mission in Japan, who himself subsequently shared the martyrs' fate, proceeded to Rome, and was heard in their cause as an eye witness.

At the same time there began to arrive petitions from those who had particular motives of interest in the process. Cardinal John Dominic Spinola, Bishop of Lucca, took it in hand as a kinsman of the martyr, and all the other members of the family addressed him letters still extant. By his intervention Father Virgil

Cepari, of the Society of Jesus, was appointed postulator of the cause. He did not confine his application to Father Spinola, but undertook the cause of several other martyrs. Then the process took another form; and, at the instance of the King of Spain and the procurators of the religious orders, Pope Urban VIII., in 1627, ordered the examination to extend to each of the martyrs named in the depositions. This took place at Manilla and Macao, and sixty depositions taken with all the formalities were transmitted to Rome.

Then discussions began. From the established facts, was there, on the part of the tyrant, what constitutes real martyrdom? This question was answered in the affirmative on 3d of February, 1687, and confirmed by Innocent XI. In the hope of resolving the same question, so far as concerned the martyrs themselves, many steps were taken at Rome by the Catholic princes, and especially by the republic of Genoa. "The story of Father Charles Spinola," said the Doge, "eclipses the noble deeds of all his ancestors. The canonization of such a man will prove a powerful motive for confidence and favor for the Christian people." Alexander VIII., successor of Innocent XI., was about to terminate the process when he died. Other obstacles arose—all remained in suspense—and the noble cause, *causa celeberrima*, as Benedict XIV. called it, seemed abandoned.

The glorification of our holy martyrs was reserved for our times. Since the solemn canonization of twenty-six Japanese martyrs in 1862, the postulators of the religious orders, supported by the suffrages of the Catholic world, labored with zeal; Father Joseph Boero, in particular, warmly urged the cause of Father Spinola and his companions. By a superior order, the sacred Congregation of Rites, presided over by Cardinal Patrizi, resumed the examination of the case, and His Holiness, Pius IX., on the 26th of February, 1867, declared that the two hundred and five martyrs justified this title on their side and that of the tyrant; and at last, on the 30th of April following, that nothing farther opposed their beatification. He, at the same time, approved four miracles, one of them due to the intercession of Blessed Spinola. The facts were these:

Petronilla Orsini, an oblate nun of the Torre di Specchi, at Rome, had been an epileptic for more than five years. She did not pass a month without an attack of her disease. Then she fell heavily; she showed life only by fearful convulsions and by foaming at her mouth. The disease thus characterized, and inveterate too, in a person over forty, was regarded by all physicians as incurable, and remedies were no longer applied. In 1628, the sick nun, having received from Father Fabius Ambrose Spinola a picture of the Venerable Charles Spinola, conceived an extraordinary confidence that she would obtain her recovery by the intercession of this servant of God. Thus disposed she addressed him a fervent prayer, and promised to perform daily certain acts of piety in his honor. From that moment she was completely delivered from her disease, and never had the slightest relapse from that to the end of her life. This was the unanimous testimony of the other sisters, of the physician and the Jesuit Father Baldelli.

The fame of this cure filled with confidence two Benedictine nuns of St. Anne's convent at Rome. One, sister Octavia Berneri, for more than a year had felt very acute pain in her bosom, where a large steel needle had run in and remained. She commended herself to the venerable Charles Spinola, and the needle came out without effort or pain, and without even leaving a wound. The other nun, sister Claudia, had a cancerous tumor on her breast. She raised blood, and no food would remain on her stomach. Extremely debilitated, and with no hope now in physicians, she invoked the venerable Charles Spinola, and that very instant recovered her health.

I close with a prodigy of another kind. In 1663, while the French were besieging Genoa, on the 18th of May, a bomb fell on the Spinola palace, penetrating to the apartment where Philip, Count of Tassarolo, was. He turned, earnestly, to the portrait of the venerable Spinola, which hung on one side. The shell, as it burst, tore everything in the room to pieces, except the man and the portrait. As to this the Count made a formal declaration.

The cause of the holy martyrs was terminated; there remained but the ceremony of Beatification. The Catholic world was invited to it as well as to the celebration of the eighteenth centenary of the martyrdom of the Prince of the Apostles. Five hundred bishops assembled at Rome, with a prodigious number of priests and eminent laymen, gathered from all parts of the world. It is not our purpose to describe, as so many have done, the festivities that took place on that occasion. We will simply add that, on the 7th of July, 1867, Charles Spinola, professed priest of the Society of Jesus, was placed in the ranks of the Blessed, with two hundred and four other martyrs.

II.—Brief of Beatification.

PIUS IX. POPE.

FOR A PERPETUAL REMEMBRANCE.

The Church, irrigated with the blood of martyrs from its very commencement, never after ceased to display wonderful examples of fortitude; and, as tyrants invented new modes of torture to shake the constancy of the soldiers of Christ, they but increased the crowns and palms of the most valiant heroes, to the eternal glory of the Church. Nor was this without a most provident design of God, namely: to show clearly that, in the most terrible struggle, Christ Jesus, the author of our faith, is present from heaven, in order as St. Cyprian wrote, to confirm and sustain in the strife his soldiers and the adherents of his name; to fight and conquer in his servants.

From 1617 to 1632 Japan was fruitful in martyrs, a hurricane of direst persecution raging against the religion of Christ, which had been happily introduced by the heralds of the gospel. For after Taicosama, Emperor of Japan, had raged with unheard-of fury, to extinguish utterly the Christian name, and in the year

1597 had put to death on the cross twenty-six valiant defenders of the true faith, his successors not only emulated his cruelty and rage, but even far surpassed it. A law was passed that no one should succor or harbor Christians, and especially priests, under penalty of exile, confiscation and death; the crosses, altars, churches and every monument of our most holy religion were, at the word of the herald, everywhere thrown down and destroyed. To try the constancy of the Christians in their faith, the most exquisite torments were employed, which the mind shudders to remember, still more to describe. Some were fixed on crosses, and then pierced through the side with a lance; others crucified with their heads down; many shamefully mutilated and cut limb from limb; many burnt by a slow fire; not a few, plunged in sulphureous or freezing waters, suffered a death of fearful agony from the prolonged pain; others, in fine, tortured, consumed by hunger, thirst, scourges, the mephitic air of dungeons, exchanged this mortal life for one of bliss and immortality.

These atrocious sufferings they bore with such an undaunted and cheerful mind, that they revived all the courage and constancy of the early martyrs of the Church. To use the words of St. Cyprian, "they stood firmer than their executioners, nor could the most cruel torments long repeated shake their immovable faith." Nor was it only priests and heralds of the gospel doctrine who stood firm and courageous in the contest, but persons of both sexes and of every condition; most eminent nobles, men of royal blood, noble matrons, tender virgins, old men worn down by age, youths, boys and girls of four years, so that this unheard-of magnanimity and constancy can be explained only by the aid of divine grace.

In this long struggle of many years more than a thousand are recorded who confirmed the Christian faith in their blood, but inquiry under the Apostolical authority could not be made as to all. In the very heat of the persecution, the necessary examinations were made only at Madrid in Spain, at Manilla in the Philippine islands, and at Macao in China. Nevertheless many credible witnesses, questioned in the usual form, gave testimony clearly establishing the truth of the martyrdom of two hundred and five heroes. In this glorious army of martyrs, many, both priests and lay brothers, belong to the religious order of the Friars Preachers of St. Dominic, the most eminent being Alphonsus Navarrete, Louis Flores, Angelo Orsucci, Francis de Morales, Alphonsus de Mena, Dominic Castellet. The religious order of Friars Minors of St. Francis glories in not a few, the most illustrious of whom are Peter of the Assumption, Peter de Avila, Richard of St. Anne, Apollinaris Franco, Francis of St. Mary, Anthony of St. Bonaventure; the religious order of Hermits of St. Augustine rejoices that many belonged to it, the most conspicuous among them being Ferdinand of St. Joseph, Peter de Zuñiga, Bartholomew Gutierrez, Vincent Carvalho. The Society of Jesus, too, is decorated with the palms of its martyrs, and among these stand forth Charles Spinola, Francis Pacheco,

Camillus Costanzo, Paul Navarro, Jerome de Angelis, and Michael Carvalho. Laymen, companions in martyrdom followed: Andrew Tocuan, Simon Quiota, and his wife Magdalen; Gaspar Cotenda, with his aunt Apollonia and Magdalen Kyota, all descended from the race of the kings of Bungo, Arima and Firando; Anthony of Corea and his wife Mary, and their children John, a boy of twelve and Peter, of three; Lucy Freitas, an octogenarian, and Dominic Georgi with his wife Elizabeth Fernandez, and their son Ignatius, a little boy of four. Of this child a most wonderful thing is narrated in the acts, that being led to the place of execution by the lictors, after beholding unmoved and without uttering a cry, his mother's head stricken off, as if exulting to be united to his mother in the confession of the faith, he offered his neck to the executioner's sword, with all his mother's alacrity, to the amazement of all the multitude crowded around. The names of the remaining martyrs will appear in a schedule attached to these letters.

After the precious death of the just in the sight of the Lord, as St. Cyprian again writes, purchasing immortality by the price of blood and receiving the crown of consummate virtue, the necessary steps were immediately taken to examine the cause; and the proceedings having been carefully examined by the Cardinals in the Sacred Congregation of Rites, our predecessor, Urban VIII., of happy memory, at the instance of the king of Spain, and the religious orders already mentioned signed the letters authorizing a formal examination under the Apostolical authority.

Accordingly, the documents containing the juridical examination were drawn up at Manilla in the Philippine islands, and at Macao, in China, and transmitted to Rome. Then, by the sanction of our predecessor, Innocent XI, a special Congregation of Rites was held on the 20th of March, 1677, in which it was determined that the first question should be put: "Whether the martyrdom was proved as regarded the tyrant." The question was discussed in another session of the same congregation, January 25, 1687, and a decree issued with the approval of our said predecessor, that "The martyrdom in this case was proved so far as regarded the tyrant." The next question to be decided was whether "The martyrdom was proved as regarded those who suffered." This question, by reason of the times and other circumstances, has remained undecided to these days. And we have said that this has come to pass most seasonably; that in this our age, deplorable alike for the religious and civil commonwealth, when the Catholic religion is more violently and perfidiously assailed by abandoned men, we may, by proposing this signal victory of Christian heroes over the tyrant, prove the divinity of our most holy religion by a new and convincing argument, and the Church justly rejoices and triumphs at the wonder of such eminent virtue.

And, then, as God in his clemency looks down upon those regions once steeped in the innocent blood of the faithful, and opens an entrance there closed for so many years on the heralds of the gospel, in order to revive those abandoned nations with salutary doctrine, revolving this in mind, We, moved by the petitions of the said orders and of the Vicars Apostolic of the countries bordering on Japan, have granted that the long interrupted examination in this cause should proceed, and adhering to the former course of judgment, we have selected a special congregation of Cardinals, versed in Sacred Rites, to bring this cause to a close after an accurate scrutiny. The twofold question was accordingly proposed: "Whether, the martyrdom being established so far as regarded the tyrant, it was so well established in regard to those that suffered, that they might proceed further." Also, what miracles or signs had been proven. Both questions were diligently discussed, and the Cardinals and prelates present, *ex officio,* gave their opinions; nevertheless we deferred confirming with our supreme judgment, until we had earnestly prayed the Father of Light to illumine our mind with the rays of his light in so momentous an affair. At length, on Tuesday after Sexagesima, a day when we recall the torments which Christ, the Lord of the human race, suffered for our salvation, we ordered a decree to be issued in these words: "I. The martyrdom on the part of those who suffered is so established that they may proceed to Beatification. II. The fourth, twelfth, thirteenth and fourteenth miracles are established."

It only remained to interrogate the Cardinals of the Sacred Congregation of Rites in the usual form, whether they deemed that we might safely proceed to enroll the venerable servants of God in the number of the Blessed. Having assembled before us on the

13th of April, they, with the concurrence of the consultors, gave an affirmative reply. Yet, before expressing our opinion, we still wished to wait in order to implore God, the author of all, to be propitious to us in the important matter, and finally on the feast of St. Catharine of Sienna, secondary patroness of Rome, we openly proclaimed that it was safe to proceed to the Beatification of the venerable servants of God.

Accordingly, at the instance of the said four religious orders and of the Apostolic Vicars who watch over the Christian flock in the regions near Japan, by the advice of our venerable brethren, the Cardinals of the Holy Roman Church, having jurisdiction over lawful rites, We, by apostolic authority, in these letters, grant that the venerable servants of God, Alphonsus Navarrete, Aloysius Flores, Angelo Orsucci, of the order of St. Dominic, Peter de Avila, Peter of the Assumption, and Richard of St. Anne, of the Friars Minor of St. Francis; Peter de Zuñiga, Ferdinand of St. Joseph, Bartholomew Gutierrez, of the order of Hermits of St. Augustine; Charles Spinola, Francis Pacheco, of the Society of Jesus; Joachim Firayama or Diaz, Lucy Fleites, and other companions in martyrdom, both religious of said orders and lay persons, be hereafter styled Blessed, and their bodies and relics be proposed to the public veneration of the faithful, solemn supplications excepted.

Moreover, by our same authority we permit that the common office and mass of several martyrs be annually recited in their honor on the designated day, according to the rubrics of the Roman Missal and Breviary. We permit the recitation of said office in the houses and churches of the said four religious orders by all the faithful, secular and regular, who are bound to recite the canonical hours, and in regard to masses, to priests officiating in churches in which the feast of the Blessed is celebrated.

We finally grant that within one year from the date of these Letters, the solemnity of the Beatification of the venerable servants of God be performed in the churches of the said orders with office and mass of double rite, and command the same to be performed on a day to be appointed by the ordinary, and after the celebration of said solemnities in our Vatican Basilica, all apostolic constructions, and Decrees of noncultus, and others whatever to the contrary notwithstanding. We wish the same credit to be given in judicial proceedings to printed copies of these letters signed by the Secretary of the said Congregation, and sealed with the seal of the Prefect, as would be given to our will expressed in these original letters.

Given at St. Peter's at Rome under the Fisherman's ring, the 7th day of May, 1867, of our Pontificate the twenty-first.

N. Cardinal Paracciani Clarelli.

COPIE DU TABLEAU EXPOSE A S.T PIERRE DE ROME

BIENHEUREUX
A. Navaret, P. d'Avila, Ch. Spinola,
P. Zuniga, J. Firayama, Th. Catenda, M.ᵉ Tacuan,
Elis.ᵗʰ Fernandez et son fils Ignace
et 196 martyrs japonais
Béatifiés le 7 Juillet 1867.

NAMES OF THE TWO HUNDRED AND FIVE MARTYRS,

BEATIFIED JULY 7, 1867,

IN CHRONOLOGICAL ORDER, FROM THE AUTHENTIC CATALOGUE ANNEXED TO THE BRIEF.

I.—May 22, 1617.

1. B. Peter of the Assumption, Spanish priest of the order of St. Francis.
2. B. John Baptist Machado de Tavora, Portuguese priest of the Society of Jesus, beheaded.

The former was betrayed by a false brother who enticed him to his house under the pretext of converting a repentant apostate. The latter was arrested in the island de Goto while hearing confessions. They cheerfully and piously spent their last days in the Omura prison, and were beheaded near it. Father Machado was only thirty-seven. Born in the island of Terceira, one of the Azores, he entered the Society of Jesus at an early age, and according to the statement of his superiors led an angelic life. Bartoli relates several miracles wrought by his intercession.

II.—June, 1617.

3. B. Alphonsus Navarrete, Spanish Dominican priest

4. B. Ferdinand of St. Joseph, Spanish Augustinian priest.

5. Leo Tanaca, Father Machado's Catechist; beheaded.

After the martyrdom of the preceding, B. Alphonsus, impelled by divine inspiration, resumed his religious habit, left Nagasaki, and going to Omura, devoted himself openly to the ministry with B. Ferdinand. They were arrested with B. Leo and beheaded on a desert rock far from spectators. B. Alphonsus was fifty-two, and had been six years in Japan.

III.—October 1, 1617.

6. B. Gaspar Fisogiro.   7. B. Andrew Gioscinda, hosts of the preceding.

IV.—August 16, 1618.

8. John of St. Martha, Spanish Franciscan priest, beheaded.

This zealous missionary was confined three years in prison with criminals, then put to death at Meaco.

V.—March 19, 1619.

9. B. John of St. Dominic, Spanish Dominican priest. Died of illtreatment in the Omura prison. See p. 166.

VI.—November 18, 1619.

10. B. Leonard Kimura, Japanese Jesuit lay brother.

11. B. Andrew Tocuan, Japanese. 12. B. Cosmas Taquea, Corean. 13. B. John Xoum, Japanese. 14. B. Dominic Giorgi, Portuguese; burnt alive.

B. Leonard was an excellent coadjutor of the Fathers, acting in cases of necessity as missionary. B. Dominic was F. Spinola's host. The other three had also harbored priests. After a long imprisonment at Nagasaki, they were brought before Gonroc and condemned to the stake. They heard the sentence with holy joy. "See," said B. Leonard to the spectators, "it is for practising and preaching the law of God that I am condemned." " I am happier," said B. Dominic, "than if they gave me the empire of Japan." Their martyrdom was a prelude to the Great Martyrdom. It took place on the same promontory and in presence of an immense crowd. B. Leonard seemed to sport with the fire. "It hardly burns," he said, and made signs to have it pushed nearer his body. They were entirely consumed, except a few bones which were cast into the sea.

VII.—NOVEMBER 29, 1619.

15. B. Bartholomew Xequi. 16. B. Anthony Kimura. 17. B. John Ivananga. 18. B. Alexis Nacamura. 19. B. Leo Nacanisci. 20. B. Michael Tascita. 21. B. Mathias Cazaca. 22. B. Romanus Matevoca, 23. B. Matthias Nacano. 24. B. John Montaiana. 25. B. Thomas Cotenda; all Japanese; beheaded.

Twelve Japanese Christians were arrested for residing near missionaries. Their life and property were offered as the price of apostacy. One fell. The rest went to the stake on the Sacred Mount in holiday garb. B. Thomas Cotenda, a relative of the king of Firando, had long led a holy life. B. Anthony Kimura was a brother of B. Leonard (No. 10).

VIII.—JANUARY 7, 1620.

26. B. Ambrose Fernandez, Portuguese Jesuit, lay brother.

Companion of B. Spinola, died in prison. See p. 166.

IX.—MAY 22, 1620.

27. B. Mathias of Arima, Japanese Catechist, tortured to death.

This excellent Catechist was specially attached to the service of Father de Couros, provincial of the Jesuits. During the persecution he readily went on dangerous errands. "If you are taken," they said one day, "will you keep your secrets." "They may tear off my flesh and break my bones before they make me reveal anything to injure the Fathers." He was true to his word. Caught with a vestment in his hands, he was put to the torture. The usual applications extorting nothing, he was forced to swallow large quantities of water, which was then forced out by pressing violently on his stomach. As they were about to renew this torture, he said: "Let me breathe, I will inform of one worth ten, a priest from Europe, from Rome, the Christian Meaco." "Who? Where?" "He is at Firando, and is called Thomas Araki;" naming a Japanese priest or ecclesiastic who had really been at Rome, but had apostatized. "Treat him as you wish to treat good priests," he added smiling, "for I will never betray one of them." On this they attacked him so furiously, that when they wished to drag him to execution he was a corpse.

X.—AUGUST 16, 1620.

28. B. Simon Quiota. 29. B. Magdalen, his wife. 30. B. Thomas Guengoro. 31. B. Mary, his wife. 32. B. James, their son; crucified.

B. Simon was an old Catechist of the Jesuits in the kingdom of Bungo, a holy old man whose supernatural power was often attested by the possessed. He was at Cocura, capital of the kingdom of Bugen, in the northern part of the island of Ximo, with his friend B. Thomas and their families, all fervent Christians when Gietciundono, the tyrant of that district, gave them the alternative, apostasy or death. They were all crucified, head down.

XI.—August 10, 1622.

33. B. Augustine Ota, Japanese Jesuit, lay brother; beheaded.

He was taken with F. Camillus Costanzo and B. Gaspar Cotenda, and taken to the prison at Ichi in Firando, where B. Flores and B. Zuñiga were already. To reward his untiring zeal he was admitted into the Society of Jesus on the eve of his martyrdom; and by a remarkable protection, of all the letters addressed by the provincial to the prisoners at Ichi only that containing the admission of this brother reached the place.

XII.—August 19, 1622.

34. B. Louis Flores, a Belgian Dominican priest.
35. B. Peter de Zuniga, a Mexican Augustinian priest.
36. B. Joachim Firaiama, Japanese, burned alive.

They were burned alive on the Sacred Mount after seeing their companions beheaded; but by an unexpected indulgence Gonroc permitted the Christians to carry off the bodies. That of B. Flores was first deposited in the house of a widow, where the Dominicans habitually officiated, then translated to the Dominican Church at Manilla. That of B. Zuñiga was sold by the executioners at a high price to Don Martin Govea, a noble Portuguese, who transported it to Macao, where it was placed in the Church of the Society of Jesus.

B. Peter de Zuñiga, son of Don Alvaro de Zuñiga, sixth viceroy of

Mexico, and Doña Teresa, marchioness of Villamarina, was born in 1585. He had labored in the Philippines as a zealous missionary for ten years. As to his arrival in Japan, see p. 183.

B. Flores was a Belgian: his real name being Fraryn. The Fraryn family was from Ath, but had been long at Antwerp, occupying the house on the corner of the Rue aux Laines and the Rue de la Vigne. At a very early age he went to Spain, and thence to Mexico, where he entered the order of St. Dominic. His change of name was doubtless made to adapt himself to those among whom he lived. Authors differ as to his age. Father Bocro makes him sixty, but he is certainly wrong as to his birthplace. Father Malpeus of Brussels, in his Palma Fidei Sacri Ordinis Fratrum Prædicatorum, does not give his age. He says he was successively an untiring laborer and a master of novices, which implies a period of several years. Father Masetti in his Italian Life of B. Flores, citing Aduarte, Historia de la Provincia del S. Rosario de Filippines, Japan y China, states that in 1609, B. Flores was exercising the ministry in New Segovia in the Philippines. However, a Register of the Cathedral of Antwerp notes the birth of Louis, son of John Fraryn-Jacommine Malders, apparently our Saint, on the 9th of April, 1589 This would make him only thirty-three at the time of his death.

Joachim Firaiama was the captain whose zeal was rewarded by his being burned alive with the missionaries whom he was conveying. His noble character never wavered. On his way from the prison to the stake, he exhorted all present, repeating in Japanese what the missionaries whispered in Spanish. On reaching the place of execution he observed that the stake to which he was to be bound was loose; with perfect calmness and simplicity he set it firm. Even amid the flames he continued to exhort all present and pray aloud.

37. B. Leo Sucheiemon. 38. B. John Foriamon. 39. B. Michael Diaz. 40. B. Mark Xinsiemon. 41. B. Thomas Coranagui. 42. B. Anthony Giamanda. 43. B. James Densei. 44. B. Lawrence Rocuiemon. 45. B. Paul Sanciqui. 46. B. John Iago. 47. Bar-

tholomew Mofioie. 48. B. John Nangata—Japanese; beheaded.

They were compromised with the last, either as passengers or sailors. Gonroc and the renegade Feizo endeavored, but in vain, to induce them to apostatize.

SEPTEMBER 10, 1622.—THE GREAT MARTYRDOM.

49. B. Francis Morales, Spanish Dominican priest: burned alive.

He had been, for twenty years, a missionary of untiring zeal in Japan. He built two churches in the kingdom of Satzuma, and a church and convent at Fuscimi, in the kingdom of Figen.

50. B. Angelo Orsucci, an Italian Dominican priest, burned alive.

He was born at Lucca, entered the order in his youth and lived with the reputation of a saint. He died at the age of forty-nine, having been four years at prison in Omura with his friend Father Spinola.

51. B. Alphonsus de Mena. 52. B. Joseph of St. Hyacinth. 53. B. Hyacinth Orfanel — Spaniards, priests of the order of St. Dominic; burned alive.

The first resembled his cousin B. Navarrete in his ardor; the second, by his eloquence and devotion to Mary, exercised great influence; the third, by his charity, was the refuge of the unfortunate.

54. B. Alexis. 55. B. Thomas. 56. B. Dominic— Japanese.

They had been catechists to the Dominicans, but in the prison were admitted to religious profession. Alexis was burned; the other two, for want of stakes, were beheaded. During the trial, the governor, struck by the beauty of Thomas and his innocent air, which gave a charm to his whole person, advised him to deny that he knew the missionaries. "How could I say that," replied the candid Thomas, "without offending God by a lie?"

57. B. Richard of St. Anne, a Belgian priest of the order of St. Francis; burned alive.

This holy martyr was born in 1585 at Ham-sur-Heure, of a worthy family called Trouvez, but having been in childhood delivered from the jaws of a wolf by the intercession of St. Anne, whom his mother invoked, he took the name of his protectress.

In 1604 he was received into the Recollect convent of Nivelles, and after many wanderings landed at the Philippines in 1611. He was only a lay brother, but was then from his virtue and talents applied to his studies and received holy orders. He was eight years in Japan, always courageous and devoted. One day he was warned to hide at once if he wished to escape the persecutors. Several Christians were waiting for him, at the house of Lucy Freitas, to make their confessions, and he would not abandon them. He remained, was captured, imprisoned for a year, and shared the triumph of his companions.

58. B. Peter de Avila, Spanish priest. 59. B. Vincent of St. Joseph, lay brothers of the order of St. Francis.

After a life spent in gaining souls to Christ, B. Peter underwent two years' imprisonment and the stake. B. Vincent had been the companion of his missionary labors.

60. B. Charles Spinola, S. J.
61. B. Sebastian Kimura, Japanese priest of the Society of Jesus; burned alive.

This excellent missionary was a nephew of the first Japanese baptized by St. Francis Xavier, and cousin of B. Leonard Kimura, Anthony Kimura and Mary Tocuan, the whole family having been apparently blessed in its head. Sebastian was the most illustrious.

He was the first Japanese priest, having been ordained at Nagasaki by Bishop Louis Cerqueira in 1601, and, of all the Japanese priests, he was the first to receive the crown of martyrdom. Born at Firando, of Christian parents, he entered the service of the Church at twelve, was educated at the seminary of Bungo, and entered the Society of Jesus at the age of nineteen. After his novitiate he was sent to instruct neophytes; he completed his studies at Macao, and on becoming a priest displayed the highest qualities of his nation, without their defects. In the prison and at the stake he was worthy of B. Spinola. He died at the age of fifty-seven.

62. B. Gonsalvo Fusai. 63. B. Anthony Chiuni. 64. B. Peter Sampo. 65. B. Michael Xumpo. 66. B. John Cioncogu. 67. B. John Acafosci. 68. B. Louis Cavara, Japanese Jesuits.

These are the seven Japanese admitted by B. Spinola to their novitiate and then to their first vows in the Society of Jesus (see page 169). They were tried Christians, most of them renouncing great worldly advantages to consecrate themselves to the service of the Church. The Sampo family held a high rank in the kingdom of Oxu, in the northern part of the island of Niphon. Thomas Acafosci had been a brilliant officer before he became a zealous catechist of Father Kimura. Gonsalvo Fusai had played a conspicuous part at the court of Bigen, as Louis Cavara had at Arima.

69. B. Leo de Satzuma, Japanese, of the order of St. Francis.

This catechist of Father Richard of St.Anne, on learning that the missionary was arrested, went and gave himself up, so as to share his fate.

70. B. Lucy de Freitas, Japanese widow; burned alive.

This illustrious widow was a model of all virtues. She was a Japanese, but married Philip de Freitas, a Portuguese. Pious from childhood she sanctified her years of widowhood by rigorous austerity and heroic acts of charity. Her house was open to the persecuted missionaries. One day learning that the apostate Feizo sought to seduce a Christian, she ran to the spot and publicly reproached him bitterly with his conduct. As the wretched man sought to intimidate her by threats, she seized the sword of a bystander; she handed it to him, saying: "Strike, and do what you will with me." When condemned to death for harboring Father Richard she drew forth the crucifix she wore on her bosom and exclaimed: "I will cheerfully die for my God." At the age of eighty she bore the torture of fire with admirable courage.

71, 72. B. Anthony Sanga and Magdalen his wife, Japanese.

Of noble birth and highly educated, Anthony had entered the novitiate of the Jesuits, but was compelled by ill health to retire. But he devoted himself with his wife to all good works. He was a good and zealous catechist. Just before his death he wrote a very touching letter to the Provincial of the Jesuits. Unable to call himself a son, he calls himself the slave of the Society, to which he owed all that he was. " I have united with its labors, as far as I could ; and since my imprisonment I have baptized thirty-two heathens, taught the prayers to a great many and encouraged my fellow-prisoners. All this I owe to the Society which instructed and formed me, as it prepared me for the death that now awaits me. . . - . Only one thing affects me—the recollection of my leaving the Society. I seem to myself like Adam driven from the earthly Paradise. . . . . Why can I not in death become again your brother? but as this is impossible, receive me at least as your most devoted slave."

His wife was beheaded, as were most of the other martyrs of this day. Of those whose names are now given little is known, except of Elizabeth Fernandez and little Ignatius.

73. B. Anthony, a Corean, catechist under the Jesuits. 74. B. Mary his wife, a Japanese. 75, 76. B. John and Peter their children, aged twelve and three. 77. B. Paul Nangasci, Japanese, burned alive. 78. B. Thecla, his wife. 79. B. Peter (seven years

old), their child. 80. B. Paul Tanaca, a Japanese. 81. B. Mary his wife. 82. B. Elizabeth Fernandez, wife of the martyr Dominic Giorgi. 83. B. Ignatius, their child, aged four (see p. 206). 84. B. Apollonias, widow, aunt of B. Gaspar Cotenda. 85, 86. B. B. Dominic Xamada and Clara his wife, Japanese. 87. B. Mary, wife of B. Andrew Tocuan, Japanese. 88. B. Agnes, wife of B. Cosmas Taquea, Japanese. 89. B. Dominic Tacano, son of B. Mathias Tacano. 90. B. Bartholomew Xichiemon. 91, 92. B. B. Damian Jamichi and his son Michael (five years old). 93. B. B. Thomas Xiquiro (aged seventy). 94. B. Rufus Iscomola. 95. B. Mary, wife of B. John Xoum. 96, 97. B. B. Clement Vom and his son Anthony. 98. B. Dominica Ongata. 99. B. Catharine, a widow 100. B. Mary Tanaura—all Japanese.

XIV.—September 11, 1622.

101. B. Gaspar Cotenda, catechist under F. Camillus Costanzo, S. J.

102. B. Francis, aged twelve, son of B. Cosmas Taquea. 103. B. Peter, aged seven, son of B. Bartholomew Xichiemon.

<small>B. Gaspar, of the family of the kings of Firando, was twenty-one years of age. Pious and well educated, he was just about to enter the Society of Jesus. B. Peter was to have been put to death with his father, but was overlooked in the confusion. The next day the judge, out of pity, wished to make the boy say he had run away: "Not at all," replied the little martyr, "I saw that nobody took any notice of me, so I went home." Threats had no avail. "I am ready to die," said he, "for some Fathers of the Society appeared to me</small>

and encouraged me to die for Jesus Christ, and to answer freely as I do." Then these martyrs were taken to the sacred mountain, still covered with the bodies and blood of the victims of the 10th. Undismayed, they joyfully mingled their blood with that of their predecessors. Their bodies were beheaded, then reduced to ashes, and these scattered to the winds.

XV.—September 12, 1622.

104. B. Thomas Zumarraga, Spanish priest. 105. B. Mancio of St. Thomas, Japanese. 106. B. Dominic, Japanese—all of the order of St. Dominic. 107. B. Apollinaris Franca, Spanish priest. 108. B. Francis of St. Bonaventura, Japanese. 109. B. Peter of St. Clare, Japanese—all of the order of St. Francis.

After the great execution of September 10, Gonroc considered himself as the special minister of the Emperor to execute prompt and terrible justice on all religious. He accordingly sent his lieutenant to Omura, to burn at the stake all who still remained in prison. Their suffering was like that of those burned at the Great Martyrdom, but more prolonged. The two Spanish Fathers conducted each his two disciples, and all died worthy of their apostolate. Four others, Paul and Mathias Faiaci, John Iquenda and Leo Suquiemon, executed at the same time, are not included in the Brief of Beatification from want of judicial proofs.

XVI.—September 15, 1622.

110. B. Camillus Costanzo, priest of Society of Jesus; burned alive.

He was born in Calabria and first served in Prince Albert's army, and was at the siege of Ostend. At the age of twenty he became a Jesuit, retaining all the energy of his first vocation. He labored usefully in the kingdom of Bugen from 1605 to 1614; he then returned to Macao, where he wrote a Japanese treatise against the Bonzes. For the last year he had, as an apostle, traversed all the western part of Japan, especially the islands depending on the king of Firando.

The inconsiderate zeal of a Japanese lady led to his arrest. Anxious to convert her husband Soiemon, a judicial officer in the island of Ikitsuki, she said: "Who knows when we shall have so favorable an opportunity again—the blessing of hearing a holy religious? Soiemon astonished, pretended to acquiesce in his wife's desire, and soon learned the missionary's retreat and his harborers. This was all he sought. B. Camillus was arrested on the 24th of April, 1622, in the island of Ucu. His trial at Firando, imprisonment in the island of Ikinoscima, and finally his martyrdom near Firando, were a repetition of those of B. Spinola. But Father Costanzo displayed, especially amid the flames, an exultation unexampled even in the annals of this persecution. Before a great number of Catholics, pagans, and even Dutch and English Protestants, he resolutely entered the place of execution and marched up to his stake. Thence, as from a pulpit, he began to address the spectators. "I am," he said, "Camillus Costanzo, an Italian, of the Society of Jesus. I am going to be burnt alive for preaching the law of the true God. . . . We are not to fear temporal but eternal death. . . . There is not means of avoiding that woe except to embrace the law of Jesus Christ.' While he thus preached the flames rose and concealed him from the spectators. A moment after they beheld him motionless, his eyes raised to heaven, in a sort of extasy. Suddenly he intoned the psalm *Laudate Dominum*, pronounced some words of exhortation, and, what seemed really prodigious, uttered exclamations of joy, and seemed transfigured with a heavenly radiance; finally, with a voice that was heard afar he chanted *Sanctus, sanctus*, and repeating for the fifth time this homage of the Seraphim, he bowed his head and expired. The testimony to these facts is abundant, and they produced an incalculable impression.

XVII.—OCTOBER 2, 1622.

111. B Louis Giaciqui, Japanese—burned alive. 112. B. Lucy his wife. 113. Their sons, B. Andrew, aged eight, and B. Francis, four years—beheaded.

B. Giaciqui was the one who planned the escape of B. Father Flores. He was put to the torture to learn the names of his accomplices, but he showed unshaken courage. His wife and children preferring death to apostasy, were first beheaded before his eyes.

XVIII.—NOVEMBER 1, 1622.

115. B. Peter Paul Navarro, Italian, priest. 116, 117. B. B. Denis Fugiscima and Peter Onizuki, scholastics of the Society of Jesus. 118. B. Clement, a Japanese in the service of F. Navarro.

B. Navarro, countryman and friend of Father Costanzo, had labored successfully in Japan for thirty-six years, when he obtained the martyr's crown. He was discovered and arrested with his three companions at Arima, where Bungodono had succeeded the apostate Michael. This prince was not then such as he subsequently appeared. He treated Father Navarro with great humanity, and even desired to save him, but had to comply with the orders of Xongun and Gonroc. The execution was fixed for the first of November. On the morning of All Saints, by the personal favor of the prince, B. Navarro was permitted to celebrate Mass and receive the vows by which B. B. Peter and Denis became members of the Society of Jesus, as well as address a last exhortation to the sobbing Christians. This took place at Scimabara, a city lying on a gulf of that name. The stakes were erected on a promontory stretching far out into the sea. There, before the eyes of a vast concourse, the four confessors underwent the fiery ordeal with heroic fortitude.

XIX.—DECEMBER 4, 1623.

119. B. Francis Galvez, a Spanish priest of the order of St. Francis. 120. B. Jerome de Angelis, an Italian priest. 121. B. Simon Jempo, a Japanese—both of the Society of Jesus.

On arriving in Japan Father de Angelis, so long the companion of Father Spinola, was sent north and penetrated to kingdoms hitherto unapproached. He was in Jedo, the new capital of Japan, when Zongun II. succeeded his father and renewed the edicts against the Christians with many threats and promises. On the information of an apostate, Father Jerome's host was arrested. The brave man refused to give any information, but the missionary, in hopes of saving his host, gave himself up. His catechist, B. Simon Jempo, refusing to abandon his master, followed his example. Some days later, B. Francis Galvez, a Franciscan missionary, was discovered and added to the two Jesuits. The confessors continued their labors even in prison, converting and baptizing forty pagans.

Many Christians were arrested at the same time, and were held subject to Xongun's decision on his return from his coronation at Meaco. "Let them be all burned alive," was the summary sentence of the prince; and fifty Christians underwent this torture in a plain without Jedo. The two religious and John Faramondo, a gentleman, were reserved to the last; they used the delay to address, in words of salvation, the spectators who crowded from the capital, then cheerfully laid down their lives to confirm their assertions. The tyrant himself took care to establish the motive of their execution. A placard bore the following: "These men are punished with death because they are Christians." However, for want of juridical statements, only three of the fifty martyrs are beatified. The bodies were, as usual, carefully guarded, but some Christians succeeded in carrying off the head of Father de Angelis, which was conveyed to Nagasaki and thence to Macao.

XX.—FEBRUARY, 22, 1624.

122. James Carvalho, Portuguese, priest of the Society of Jesuits, frozen to death.

While the Christians were thus treated, Masamune, King of Oxu, was at the court of Jedo. Hitherto he had shown an inclination to the Christian faith, and had sent an embassy to Europe ; but, led away by the emperor's example, he ordered the governor of Scendai, his capital, to hunt down the Christians, and put all to death who refused to apostatize. Twenty-three suffered, but the necessary information could be obtained only as to the most illustrious of them, B. James Carvalho. This worthy missionary had spent his best years in Japan ; after establishing a mission at Cochin China, during his exile, he returned to Japan and joined B. Jerome de Angelis in his laborious northern mission. Tracked by Masamune's emissaries, Carvalho, warned of the danger, retired, with sixty Christians, far from all abodes, in a valley, hidden away in the mountains. They would probably have eluded pursuit, except for their footprints in the snow, which guided the persecutors. As soon as the holy missionary saw that he was discovered, he went forward to meet them, and thus gave a number of Christians time to scatter and escape.

The prisoners were led to Scendai, through the snow-blocked roads and the bitter cold. Two old men, unable to keep up, were killed by the guard. At the capital an entirely new punishment was devised for the rest. A river flowed at the foot of the fortress. On its banks a hole, several feet square, was dug, and filled with water from the river. Here the Father, with eight companions, was exposed, naked, to the torture of ice-water, amid the railleries and jeering exhortations of the pagans. After the lapse of three hours, when their limbs were numbed, they were, by order of the court, taken out. It was supposed that this first torture would make them more compliant. As the holy confessor's replies expressed only desire to sacrifice himself in so good a cause, he was taken back to the pit, plunged in the water to his knees, then to his neck, taken out, plunged in again, till he was completely frozen. He lived thus three hours, and, with his last breath, uttered the holy names of Jesus and Mary.

XXI.—August 25, 1624.

123. B. Michael Carvalho, Portuguese, priest of the Society of Jesus. 124. B. Peter Vasquez, Spaniard, Dominican priest. 125. B. Louis Sotelo, Spaniard, and 126. B. Louis Sosanda, Japanese, both priests of the order of St. Francis; and 127. B. Louis Baba, Japanese Catechist of the same order: all burned alive.

From his prison in Omura, resembling B. Spinola's B. Michael Carvalho wrote: "We are all feeble and infirm in body, but sustained and consoled in spirit, for God grants his favors in proportion to sufferings. If it please his Sovereign Majesty that I die in this prison, devoured by vermin and covered by filth, His will be done." After enduring this torment for a year and a half, they were taken from Omura to Scimabara, where they were burned. The executioner, wishing to fix the rope on one of the stakes, used the body of B. Vasquez as a footstool—mounting on his shoulders—without the martyr's resenting it. After two hours B. Louis Baba's bonds were consumed, and that good religious went and kissed the hands of B. Vasquez and Sotelo, and expired at their feet. On this occasion even the Bonzes paid homage to the courage of the martyrs, and acknowledged that God alone could raise feeble mortals to that height.

XXII.—November 15, 1624.

128. B. Caius, a Corean, Catechist to the Jesuits, burnt alive.

Born in Corea, and still a pagan, he begged God to save his soul; and God showed him an aged man, who in another land would teach him the way of salvation. Brought to Japan as a prisoner of war, he was instructed by the Jesuit missionaries, aided them in their ministry, and in reward received the martyr's crown. He was burned alive at Nagasaki, by Gonroc's order.

XXIII.—June 20, 1626.

229. Francis Pacheco, Portuguese priest. B. Balthasar de Torres, Spanish priest. 131. B. John Baptist Zola, Italian priest. 132. B. Peter Rinscei, Japanese. 133. B. Vincent Caum, Corean. 134. B. John Chinasco. 135. B. Paul Scinsuche. 136. B. Michael Tozo. 137. B. Gaspar Sadamatzu, Japanese—all of the Society of Jesus, burned alive.

In 1626 the emperor published new edicts of unheard-of severity. Every practice of the Christian religion, and even the use of the European calendar, was punished with death, and, to execute these acts, an army of spies was organized.

The first to fall into the tyrant's hands was B. Francis Pacheco, provincial of the Jesuits and administrator of the diocese. For easier communication he had remained at Cocinotzu, a port in the kingdom of Arima. He was taken, with several others of his order, to Scimabara, and shut up in a dungeon in the fortress. B. Balthasar de Torres, and Michael Tozo, his catechist, were soon after taken near Nagasaki, and imprisoned at Omura. The two parties, all Jesuits, were then sent to Nagasaki, and met at the foot of the sacred mountain, where they saluted and embraced one another with the most lively joy, amid the applause of the Christians and wonder of the pagans. It was the Great Martyrdom renewed.

XXIV.—July 12, 1626.

138. B. Mancio. 139. B. Mathias Arachi. 140. B. Peter Arachi Cobioia. 141. B. Susanna, his wife. 142-3. B. B. John Tanaca, and Catharine his wife. 144-5. B.B. John Naisen, and Monica his wife. 146. Louis, their son, seven years old—all Japanese—burned or beheaded.

After the religious, their hosts were arraigned. Cavaci, the new governor of Nagasaki, ordered them all to be put to death. He first subjected them to fearful tortures. The ladies were exposed to the insults of the mob. Susanna was hung by her hair to a tree for eight hours. Monica and Catharine were forced to swallow and then eject great quantities of water: all were thrown into loathsome dungeons. Mancio died there, but his body was burned with the rest on the Holy Mountain of Nagasaki. The ladies, with little Louis, were beheaded. The young martyr was taken to execution in a soldier's arms. When set down, not understanding all the preparations, he ran to his mother, who, absorbed in the thought of her approaching death, pushed him away, exciting his grief and surprise. His father, perceiving it from his stake said: "Grieve not, Louis; in a few moments we shall all three be re-united in heaven." All the martyrs died in similar sentiments. One of them, John Tanaca, an aged man, did what was deemed miraculous. Seeing his bonds consumed, he left his stake and went to each martyr, saluting them, kissing their hands, praising God for their constancy, passing through the burning coals as if he were incombustible. He then went back to his stake and died praying.

XXV.—July 29, 1627.

147. B. Louis Bertrand, priest. 148. B. Mancio, of the Holy Cross; and 149. B. Peter of St. Mary—both Japanese—all of the order of St. Dominic: burned alive.

B. Louis Bertrand, a nephew of St. Louis Bertrand, the apostle of South America, was burned at Omura, with two fervent Catechists of his order. This is about all we know of their martyrdom, the narratives being less detailed as the times grew more difficult.

XXVI.—August 16, 1627.

150. B. Francis Curobioje, and 151. B. Caius Je-

11

mon, Japanese, beheaded. 152. B. Magdalen Chiota, related to the king of Bungo, burned. 153. B. Francis, Japanese, burned. 154. B. Francis of St. Mary, a Spaniard, priest of the order of St. Francis; with 155. B. Bartholomew Laurel, a Mexican; and 156. B. Anthony, of St. Francis, a Japanese, his Catechist of the same order, burned alive. 157. B. Gaspar Voz, Japanese, beheaded. 158. B. Thomas Vo, Japanese, beheaded. 159. B. Francis Enfioie, Japanese, burned. 160. B. Luke Chiemon; 161. B. Michael Chizaiemon; 162. B. Louis Matzuo; 163. B. Martin Gomez; and 164. B. Mary—all Japanese—beheaded.

XXVII.—September 7, 1627.

165. B. Thomas Tzugi, Japanese priest, of the Society of Jesus; 166. B. Louis Maqui; and 167. B. John, his son—Japanese; all burned alive.

B. Thomas Tzugi, born on the territory of Omura, was educated in the seminary of Arima, and, entering the Society, became a very distinguished preacher. In the worst times of the persecution he assumed all sorts of disguises to sustain the faithful, and especially that of porter; but one day his courage failed him, and he asked to withdraw from the Society of Jesus. He had scarcely received his dismission when he repented, and asked to re-enter the order. Having no complaint to make of him, the superiors merely subjected him to fresh trials, and God, having permitted this humiliation, gave him the opportunity to repair his fault by martyrdom. His hosts shared his triumph.

XXVIII.—September 8, 1628.

168. B. Anthony of St. Bonaventure, Spanish priest,

and 169. B. Dominic, of Nagasaki, both Franciscans. 170. B. Dominic Castellet, Spanish priest; 171. B. Thomas, of St. Hyacinth, and 172. B. Anthony, of St. Dominic, Japanese, all Dominicans. 173. John Tomachi, with his four sons. 174. B. Dominic (sixteen years old). 175. B. Michael, (thirteen years). 176. B. Thomas, (ten years). 177. B. Paul, (seven years). 178. B. John Imamura. 179. B. Paul Aibara. 180. B. Romanus. 181. B. Leo. 182. B. James Faiascida. 183. B. Matthew Alvarez. 184. B. Michael Jamada, and 185. B. Lawrence, his son. 186. B. Louis Nisaci, with his sons. 187. B. Francis (five years), and 188. B. Dominic, (two years). 189. B. Louisa, aged eighty —all Japanese : twelve burned, ten beheaded.

Religious and harborers of religious, they were martyred at Nagasaki by order of Bungodono, prince of Omura, who had become a violent persecutor. The religious, with their chief hosts, were burned. One of them has left us this noble expression : "Now I see that I am thine, O my Jesus!" As usual the beheading took place first. The heads of B. Tomachi's four sons were thrown on his fire and consumed with him. Amid their trials these noble Christians chanted the praises of God.

XXIX.—September 16, 1628.

190. B. Michael Fimonoia. 191. B. Paul Fimonoia. 192. B. Dominic Xobioie, beheaded at Nagasaki.

XXX.—December 25, 1628.

193. B. Michael Nacascima, Japanese Jesuit, applied to "The Mouths of Hell."

From childhood B. Michael led an exemplary life. At a later day he took part in all the works of zeal that the persecution surrounded with greatest peril. After his admission into the Society of Jesus, he bore, with heroic constancy, all that the tyranny of his persecutors could invent. He was first bastinadoed at the mercy of his executioners, then subjected, on different occasions, to the torture of water, used in the most brutal manner; finally, they had recourse, for the first time, to a new torture.

Some leagues from Arima, stands Mount Ungen, with three summits, separated by fissures, from which issue boiling waters and sulphurous exhalations. These waters corrupt and decompose the flesh; the effluvia they emit is enough to extinguish life. Hence they were called "Mouths of Hell!"

To use them against the Christians required some skill. The persecutor had no idea of stifling them instantly. They were passed through some basins where the water was only kneedeep; then covered with boiling water and gradually plunged into the deepest fissures. When they could bear no more they were withdrawn. Thus was B. Michael Nacascima boiled to pieces, no word escaping his lips except the names of Jesus and Mary. He knew by experience the efficacy of this invocation, for in a letter written after his first torture to Father Emanuel de Borges, we read: "When the pain became too intense, I invoked Our Lady the Blessed Virgin, and my pain instantly ceased."

XXXI.—SEPTEMBER 28, 1630.

194. B. John Cocumbuco. 195. B. Mancio. 196. B. Michael Chinosci. 197. B. Lawrence Scixo. 198. B. Peter Cufioie. 199. B. Thomas, all of the third order of St. Augustine, beheaded.

Between 1629 and 1632 there were more than three hundred martyrs, but positive information could be obtained only as to six. God knows and crowns all.

XXXII.—September 3, 1632.

200. B. Bartholomew Guttierez, Mexican priest. 201. B. Vincent Carvalho, Portuguese priest. 202. B. Francis of Jesus, Spanish priest, all three Augustinians. 203. B. Anthony Iscida, Japanese priest of the Society of Jesus. 304. B. Jerome de Torres, Japanese priest. 205. B. Gabriel of Magdalen, Spanish Franciscan.

From 1629 Tachimaga Uneme, successor to Cavaci, governor of Nagasaki, and commissary of the Emperor in all Southern Japan, undertook by every means to extirpate Christianity. He exhausted the patience of the Christians by prolonged tortures, and attacked them in every way most repugnant to their instincts. He forced the men to go on all fours like brutes through filth; he exposed the women stripped to the insults of the mob, and other atrocities. It must be admitted that the number of apostates then increased. No succor could reach them, and tyranny developed an infernal system. After terror came stratagem. Uneme pretended to relax. He took the air of one who felt that it was all over and the Christians extirpated. At the same time he watched all suspected spots, and soon captured several priests on whom he resolved to try every means of seduction, and if he failed, every species of torment. He was bent especially on obtaining the apostacy of the Japanese, above all of one like B. Anthony Iscida, a Jesuit and priest as well. But all his arts, all his offers failed to move the holy religious. Then he had recourse to the "Mouths of Hell," and employed them with refinements of cruelty. Each martyr was taken thither separately; each subjected to the torture of the devouring waters as far as his strength permitted. The strongest were tortured six times a day; a physician daily applying remedies till they were able to begin again. This torture lasted a month, not a martyr quailed. The tyrant was defeated, and the whole city of Nagasaki proclaimed the heroism of the martyrs of Jesus Christ. Uneme, to conceal his defeat, had them secretly conveyed to the Sacred Mountain and there privately burned.

Such are the two hundred and five martyrs whose process could be regularly conducted. Of these seventy-eight were members of religious orders in the strict sense, being priests, catechists or tertiaries. St. Dominic numbers twenty-one children; St. Francis, eighteen; St. Augustine, five; and St. Ignatius, thirty-four.

These were not the last martyrs. The persecution continued to immolate the Japanese by hundreds; and from 1632 to 1646 seven more Dominicans, two Franciscans, two Augustinians, and forty Jesuits were put to death for the faith, some by fire, others by the horrible torture of the pit. Even later it was not fear that arrested the missionaries; but the impossibility of penetrating into Japan, without trampling on the image of Jesus crucified. The country was closed, till the moment God had set apart to pour down his favors on the descendants of so many noble martyrs.

B. SPINOLA'S PRACTICE OF DEVOTION

IN HONOR OF THE

BLESSED VIRGIN, MOTHER OF GOD.

This practice consists in honoring Mary specially as Mother of God, and glorifying the privileges she enjoys under that title. He marks nine privileges corresponding to the nine months between the Annunciation and Christmas. Each privilege is the subject of 1st. A short consideration; 2d. A homage rendered to Mary—Hail Mary; 3d. A prayer analogous to the Consideration.

I. PRIVILEGE.—Mary, Mother of God, really conceived the Eternal Word by the operation of the Holy Ghost. I will render thanks to God, and conceive the most profound respect for his Blessed Mother. Let me, O my God, by submission to thy holy will, in some sort partake of this privilege, according to the words of the gospel: "Whosoever doeth the will of my Father, who is in heaven, he is my brother, my sister, and my mother."

II. PRIVILEGE.—To Divine Maternity, Mary added Virginity. She renounced the most august dignity, rather than consent to forego her virginity.

Grant me by her merits, O Jesus, to perish a thousand times rather than lose purity of heart.

III. PRIVILEGE.—The presence of Jesus in Mary, far from being a burthen, alleviated all pain and tribulation.

May thy yoke thus be ever light to me, O Jesus, that I may walk courageously in the path of thy commandments.

IV. Privilege.—Mary having no share in the fall of Eve, brought forth her Son without pain.

Obtain for me, O august Mother of God, that, rousing from my sloth, I may produce in joy abundant fruits of salvation.

V. Privilege.—With the author of all good, Mary received the plenitude of Grace, raising her above all the Saints. Implore our Lord by the merits of His Holy Mother to expand your heart and prepare it to receive and employ the graces he has laid up for you.

VII. Privilege.—The Eternal Word after assuming our flesh in the womb of the Blessed Virgin, as High Priest consecrated it as the living Temple of the Divinity, and the Most High has sanctified his tabernacle. By a less august but real title you are the temple of the Holy Ghost: respect it and implore God, through Mary ever to preserve you free from stain.

VII. Privilege.—Mary's womb is the precious vase containing the bread of life, our Spiritual food. She invites you to share it with her. May you, by her intercession, relish it with her, and ever increase in virtue and merit.

VIII. Privilege.—By the ineffable communications of the second Adam, Mary has become a second Eve, the happy mother of the true living, the children of God. Entertain for her the sentiments of a pious child, a boundless confidence, and an immense desire to resemble your Mother.

IX. Privilege.—Honored by the presence of God and his attendant angels, the humble virgin is transformed into a paradise, illumined with heavenly splendors.

Obtain for me, O Mary, a like transformation; and above all, help me to pluck from the garden of my heart the thorns and brambles, help me to make straight and level the ways of the Lord.

CONTENTS.

	PAGE
PREFACE	3
INTRODUCTION	7

PART I.

PREPARATION FOR THE APOSTLESHIP.

I.—The desire of Blessed Charles for Martyrdom	49
II.—His Vocation to the Society of Jesus	54
III.—Fervor of the Young Novice	57
IV.—The Student's Twofold Progress	62
V.—His First Mission as a Priest	67
VI.—Preparations for his Departure for Japan	70

PART II.

VOYAGES OF BLESSED CHARLES SPINOLA.

I.—His Apostleship at Sea	74
II.—Mission of Porto Rico	83
III.—A Prisoner in England	92
IV.—Arrival of Blessed Charles in Japan	103

PART III.

APOSTOLIC LIFE IN JAPAN.

I.—State of the Mission	110
II.—Commencement of his Labors in Japan	117
III.—His Pastoral Functions	120
IV.—His Domestic Offices	124
V.—The Great Persecution	133
VI.—Secret Missions of Blessed Charles Spinola	141

PART IV.

MARTYRDOM.

	PAGE
I.—The Examination	150
II.—The Prison	158
III.—Behavior of the Holy Prisoner	167
IV.—Removal to Firando	183
V.—The Condemnation	189

PART V.

BEATIFICATION.

I.—Examination of the Case 210
II.—Brief of Beatification 215

Account of the two hundred and five Martyrs 226
B. Charles Spinola's Practice of Devotion 247

www.ingramcontent.com/pod-product-compliance
Lightning Source LLC
Chambersburg PA
CBHW031727230426

43669CB00007B/277